Public Finances, Stabilization and Structural Reform in Latin America

Guillermo Perry
Ana María Herrera

Published by the Inter-American Development Bank
Distributed by The Johns Hopkins University Press

Washington, D.C.
1994

The views and opinions expressed in this publication are those of the authors and do not necessarily reflect the official position of the Inter-American Development Bank.

**Public Finances, Stabilization and Structural Reform in
Latin America**

Inter-American Development Bank
1300 New York Avenue, N.W.
Washington, D.C. 20577

Distributed by
The Johns Hopkins University Press
2715 North Charles Street
Baltimore, MD 21218-4319

Library of Congress Catalog Card Number: 94–73299

ISBN: 0–940602–92–X

PROLOGUE

This book offers an important contribution to the policy debate regarding public finance in Latin America and the Caribbean. In addition, recognizing that the management of public finances has a direct effect on a number of other policy decisions, the authors provide an overview of related issues involving economic reform (including stabilization, structural reform, trade liberalization, and tax reform) as well as reform of the State (such as privatization and fiscal decentralization).

Research for this book was conducted under the auspices of the Visiting Scholars Program within the Integration and Regional Programs Department at the Inter-American Development Bank. Under this program, scholars come and share their experience with the Bank's technical units and provide greater understanding of the region's development needs by carrying out applied research projects that result in works such as the present volume.

The analysis done by Guillermo Perry, in collaboration with Ana María Herrera, comes at a very opportune moment in the region's development process, as governments strive to maintain support for the reforms made over the last few years. Eventually, as more citizens begin to realize the benefits of paying their taxes, workers who are currently involved in the informal sector will become important contributors to the well-being of society. Meanwhile, however, the people of Latin America and the Caribbean will be keeping a close eye on fiscal affairs, making sure that their taxes are being efficiently managed and equitably distributed. Herein lies one of the region's greatest challenges in the immediate future.

Nohra Rey de Marulanda
Manager
Integration and Regional Programs Department

FOREWORD

The past decade has been a remarkable one for the economies of Latin America. Ten years ago the continent was in the grip of a major debt crisis. In most countries the inflation rate was high, public finances were in a mess, growth prospects were poor, output was down, and the servicing of the heavy debt burden absorbed a large share of export earnings, precluding any optimism for the future. It is not surprising, therefore, that the 1980s came to be referred to as the "lost decade."

Several factors contributed to this situation, some domestic and some external (or exogenous, as economists would put it). The external factors primarily included the sharp increase in real interest rates and the declining terms of trade experienced by many of these countries as commodity prices slid from the high levels reached in the 1970s. The increasing cost of servicing their debt, along with the reduction of income that these countries earned from their export activities, combined to worsen the region's balance of payments difficulties. The internal factors included poor policies, which often originated from the overambitious role assigned to the public sector, a role that could not be fully financed from the revenue generated by the inefficient tax system. When that role was exercised through regulations instead of spending, it naturally aggravated the distortion of these economies. Thus, Latin American economies were suffering from major macroeconomic imbalances and the widespread inefficiencies associated with the policies followed by populist governments over the years.

Toward the end of the 1980s, remarkable changes started to take place in several Latin American countries. Less ideological leaders, who either had better training or a better understanding of economics, came into power in several of these countries. These individuals started addressing the major distortions that had been afflicting these countries. They addressed these difficulties with dedication and a clarity of purpose that was new and refreshing. In their attempts to improve economic conditions, they cast aside dogmas and introduced policies that were more in tune with the basic laws of economics. Macroeconomic imbalances and economic distortions were reduced. Within a few years the clouds that had threatened the continent started lifting. Although not all the countries have benefitted from the same improvements, and not all the problems have been solved, in many Latin American countries the economic problems that remain seem more manageable than they did in the 1980s.

These improvements have been particularly impressive in the area of fiscal policy. This is important because many of the difficulties of the early period could be traced to, or at least were closely connected with, the large fiscal imbalances. Large fiscal deficits financed by monetary expansions had led to inflationary pressure and major distortions in external economic relations. In many of these countries, fiscal deficits and balance of payments difficulties had gone hand-in-hand.

This book provides an interesting, careful, and well articulated description and analysis of many of these developments. It focuses especially on the connection between macroeconomic imbalances and developments in public finance and analyzes the channels through which overvalued exchange rates reduced tax revenue by reducing tax bases. The six chapters that make up this book are packed with detailed information that is not easily available elsewhere. The authors have marshalled this information in order to develop their analysis concerning the connection between fiscal adjustment and general improvements in the economies and to deal with specific topics such as the fiscal impact of both decentralization and privatization. They show that the relationship between macroeconomic improvements and fiscal adjustment runs both ways. Fiscal developments clearly affect economic developments, but macroeconomic developments also affect fiscal developments. This is an important message that is too often forgotten or even ignored.

Guillermo Perry brings with him plenty of policy experience and technical sophistication, both of which are necessary ingredients for producing this kind of book. He also brings to the task a background rooted in both macroeconomics and public finance, a combination that is not too common. The Inter-American Development Bank deserves credit for having sponsored this research. Economic policy is improved when the lessons learned from particular countries are available to the policymakers of other countries. In this way the latter have a better chance of avoiding mistakes. It is important for institutions such as the IDB, which try to assist countries in improving their policymaking, to support activities that help with the diffusion of these lessons. This book will prove very valuable to scholars and policymakers alike, and the IDB can be proud of its contribution to this activity.

Vito Tanzi
Director
Fiscal Affairs Department
International Monetary Fund

CONTENTS

INTRODUCTION*

Most Latin American countries experienced exchange and fiscal crises in the early 1980s. These crises were the result of simultaneous external shocks (terms of trade deterioration, the rise of international interest rates, and the subsequent suspension of external commercial bank credit), growing macroeconomic disequilibria, and the accumulation of considerable external debt facilitated by the ease of obtaining international financial resources in the second half of the 1970s. Governments responded with adjustment and stabilization programs, which varied both in terms of intensity and success. To date (1992), many Latin American countries have achieved their macroeconomic equilibrium and stabilization goals, but not all have managed to overcome the effects that the crisis and the adjustment programs had on the rates of investment and economic growth.

Concurrent with the macroeconomic adjustment in some cases—and either before or after it in others—most of the countries of Latin America instituted structural reforms aimed at greater international competitiveness in their productive sectors. A growing number of countries have implemented programs involving trade and financial liberalization, the deregulation of domestic markets, the privatization of public enterprises, and other government reforms that have had a significant impact on their public finances.

The aim of this study is to extract the most important lessons taught by these experiences with respect to the management of public finances and of taxation systems in particular. The analysis is based on the study of four countries—Argentina, Chile, Colombia, and Mexico—that have carried out structural reform processes at various points in time and have managed, some before others, to adjust their public finances and to implement successful stabilization programs. Occasionally, however, the findings of other studies are used to provide a broader view of the current trends in the region.

---

*This study benefitted from the comments of Vito Tanzi and Richard Bird, which were provided at the presentation of a preliminary version at the IDB, as well as those of Eduardo Lora and Gary McMahon.

In the first chapter, we examine the dynamics of the public finance crisis of the first half of the 1980s, analyzing the erosion effect that external shocks, the autonomous variables of fiscal policy, and the internal economic crisis had on public finances during that period. Thereafter follows an analysis of the fiscal adjustment processes and the contribution of exogenous, endogenous, and autonomous variables to the success or failure of such adjustment. The chapter concludes with an overview of the trends observed in the last two decades in public finance and taxation systems in the four countries studied. In particular, an explanation is given for the reversal of the deterioration in broad-based taxes during most of the last decade (particularly the income tax, but also the value-added tax [VAT] in some countries) as well as the shift in the initial emphasis of the adjustment programs on social spending cuts, public investment and raising minor taxes in the four countries studied since the late 1980s or early 1990s.

Chapter Two analyzes the role of public finances and fiscal policy in the stabilization programs. The review of this experience leaves no doubt about the importance of fiscal adjustment to the success of stabilization programs. It is also noted that fiscal equilibrium or adjustment and the trend of inflation rates are not always closely related.

This lack of correlation is due to three factors, the implications of which are analyzed in detail throughout the chapter. First, the heavy reliance of public finances on revenue from major export products observed in three of the four countries indicates an anticyclical, endogenous trend in the performance of public finances. This phenomenon requires the formulation and implementation of appropriate exchange and fiscal stabilization measures. The second factor is the high degree of inflationary inertia, due both to the shortening of the term of contracts and the generalization of indexation clauses and procedures. This set of circumstances rendered traditional stabilization programs inefficient, led to fluctuations in the real exchange rate (and in other relative prices generally), had a substantial impact on inflation rates, and required the implementation of "unorthodox" stabilization programs. Finally, some countries accumulated considerable public debt as a consequence of persistent fiscal and quasi-fiscal deficits during most of the period. Given the many factors associated with this outstanding debt (including devaluation, inflation, and the debt repudiation expectations of private agents), fiscal adjustment, the anchoring of the exchange rate, and the application of price and wage policies proved inadequate, and it became necessary to find ways of alleviating the debt burden.

Chapter Two also contains an analysis of the exchange and fiscal dilemmas recently faced by the most open of the four economies as a result of heavy inflows of private capital in the early 1990s. The chapter also examines the differential impact that the crises and adjustment programs had on investment and growth rates in the sample countries.

Chapter Three presents a discussion of the fiscal impact of trade liberalization, both from a theoretical perspective and through specific analysis of the experiences of the four countries studied. In this connection, a detailed description is given of the characteristics of their protective trade systems as well as the content and sequence of the liberalization processes that made it possible in three of the four countries for the trade reform not to have a negative initial impact on public finances, even though it may become necessary in all of them to replace taxes on foreign trade with taxes on domestic activities. The analysis highlights the unusual situation of the smaller countries of the region, which requires unconventional solutions.

Chapter Four examines the impact of two public finance reforms (the process of decentralization and intergovernmental finance reform and the privatization process), identifies certain critical topics, raises various concerns, and offers a number of related proposals.

In conclusion, Chapter Five specifically identifies the trends of the tax reforms carried out in the countries of the region in the last two decades, as well as their relationship to the processes of structural adjustment, particularly trade and financial deregulation. The chapter also investigates the analytical and political aspects revealed by these trends, which will dominate the study of tax policies in Latin America in this decade.

As it unfolds, this study brings to light the common characteristics not only of the dynamic of disequilibrium and subsequent macroeconomic and fiscal adjustment, but also of the long-term trends of public finance and taxation systems in the region. However, it also demonstrates the influence of the differences in initial conditions, economic structure, and specific management of economic and fiscal policy in the four countries studied. The chapter therefore concludes with recommendations concerning the various aspects analyzed, which apply to other countries of the region as well, and points out the necessity of finding solutions adapted to the specific conditions—both structural and cyclical—of each economy.

CHAPTER ONE

TREND OF
PUBLIC FINANCES

The Fiscal Crisis in the Early 1980s

Most of the countries of Latin America had serious fiscal deficits in the first half of the 1980s, which was part of the general economic decline that occurred during this period, and most of them implemented adjustment programs with varying degrees of intensity and success. Throughout the decade, the consolidated deficits of the nonfinancial public sector exceeded 4 percent of gross domestic product (GDP) in the 13 countries included in Table 1.1, 7 percent in 10 of them and 10 percent in five (Argentina, Bolivia, Mexico, Peru, and Uruguay). Adding the deficit generated by quasifiscal operations, the consolidated deficit topped 20 percent of GDP in Argentina in 1983 and in Mexico in 1986 and 1987 (Table 1.2). The extent of the subsequent adjustment is made especially clear by observing the trend of the primary balance of the nonfinancial public sector (excluding interest payments). Eight of the countries in Table 1.1 had primary fiscal surpluses at the close of the decade.

The erosion of public finances was largely the result of the external shocks sustained by the economies of the region early in the decade, particularly the deterioration of the terms of trade and the rise of international interest rates. This erosion was also due to the considerable accumulation of external debt as a consequence of the growing current account deficits in the latter half of the 1970s and the early 1980s and, in many cases, to the application of expansive fiscal policies since the late 1970s.

Table 1.1. Consolidated Surplus (Deficit) of the Nonfinancial Public Sector
(Percentages of GDP)

	1980	Maximum deficit	Year	1990	1991
Argentina					
Total surplus (deficit)	8.0	−17.9	(1983)	−5.1	−1.6
Primary surplus (deficit)	−4.6	−11.9		−2.0	0.4
Bolivia					
Total surplus (deficit)	−7.8	−26.6	(1984)	−8.3[a]	n.a.
Primary surplus (deficit)	−5.2			−6.3[a]	n.a.
Brazil					
Total surplus (deficit)	−2.0	−7.4	(1988)	−7.4[b]	n.a.
Primary surplus (deficit)	0.0			−1.1[b]	n.a.
Chile					
Total surplus (deficit)	5.6	−4.4	(1984)	5.3[c]	n.a.
Primary surplus (deficit)	6.4	−2.0		7.5[c]	n.a.
Colombia					
Total surplus (deficit)	−2.3	−7.4	(1983)	−0.7	n.a.
Primary surplus (deficit)	−0.8	−5.2		3.0	n.a.
Costa Rica					
Total surplus (deficit)	−9.3	−9.3	(1980)	3.3[a]	n.a.
Primary surplus (deficit)	−3.1			9.6[a]	n.a.
Ecuador					
Total surplus (deficit)	−7.4	−8.5	(1981)	−4.4[a]	n.a.
Primary surplus (deficit)	−4.3			−0.5[a]	n.a.
Guatemala					
Total surplus (deficit)	−4.7	−7.4	(1981)	−1.3[a]	n.a.
Primary surplus (deficit)	−4.1			0.1[a]	n.a.
Mexico					
Total surplus (deficit)	−6.9	−16.8	1982)	−7.6[c]	n.a.
Primary surplus (deficit)	−3.4	−8.6		5.4[c]	n.a.
Paraguay					
Total surplus (deficit)	1.3	−4.9	(1984)	−0.9[b]	n.a.
Primary surplus (deficit)	1.8			0.5[b]	n.a.
Peru					
Total surplus (deficit)	−3.9	−10.3	(1983)	−5.5[c]	n.a.
Primary surplus (deficit)	0.8			−3.8[c]	n.a.
Uruguay					
Total surplus (deficit)	1.3	−10.4	(1982)	0.7[a]	n.a.
Primary surplus (deficit)	1.8			3.2[a]	n.a.
Venezuela					
Total surplus (deficit)	7.3	−5.5	(1988)	−5.5[b]	n.a.
Primary surplus (deficit)	10.8			−1.7*	n.a.

n.a. = not available
[a] Figure for 1987.
[b] Figure for 1988.
[c] Figure for 1989.
Sources: 1990 Economic Survey of Latin America and the Caribbean, ECLAC. Case studies.

Table 1.2. Public Sector Surplus (Deficit)
(Percentages of GDP)

	1980	1981	1982	1983	1984	1985	1986	1987	1988	1989	1990	1991
Chile[1]												
Consolidated public sector	n.a.	n.a.	-8.8	-7.1	-9.2	-8.8	-4.8	-1.7	1.9	n.a.	n.a.	n.a.
Financial public sector (quasifiscal)	n.a.	n.a.	-5.3	-4.3	-4.8	-7.3	-2.9	-1.3	-0.6	n.a.	n.a.	n.a.
Nonfinancial public sector	5.6	0.8	-3.5	-2.8	-4.4	-2.5	-1.9	-0.4	2.5	5.3	2.7	n.a.
Interest payments	0.8	0.4	0.6	1.8	2.4	3.2	2.4	2.9	3.0	2.2	2.3	n.a.
Primary	n.a.	n.a.	-2.9	-1.0	-2.0	0.7	0.5	2.5	5.5	7.5	5.0	n.a.
Colombia												
Consolidated public sector	-2.3	-4.7	-6.5	-8.5	-6.8	-5.4	-1.4	-3.0	-3.3	n.a.	n.a.	n.a.
Financial public sector (quasifiscal)	0.0	0.8	-0.5	-1.0	-0.9	-1.0	-1.1	-1.1	-0.8	n.a.	n.a.	n.a.
Nonfinancial public sector	-2.3	-5.5	-6.0	-7.4	-5.9	-4.4	-0.3	-1.9	-2.5	-2.4	-0.7	-0.5
Interest payments	1.5	1.6	1.9	2.2	2.6	3.2	3.3	4.0	3.8	3.9	3.7	3.7
Primary	-0.8	-3.9	-4.1	-5.2	-3.4	-1.2	3.0	2.1	1.3	1.5	3.0	3.2
Mexico[2]												
Consolidated public sector	-8.4	-13.1	-15.1	-13.1	-11.3	-12.3	-22.4	-23.9	-13.9	-6.8	n.a.	n.a.
Financial public sector (quasifiscal)[3]	-1.4	0.4	1.7	-3.1	-2.1	-2.5	-5.5	-7.5	-2.3	0.8	n.a.	n.a.
Nonfinancial public sector	-6.9	-13.5	-16.8	-10.0	-9.2	-9.8	-16.9	-16.5	-11.6	-7.8	n.a.	n.a.
Interest payments	3.5	5.0	8.2	12.4	11.9	11.5	16.6	19.7	16.7	13.0	n.a.	n.a.
Primary	-3.4	-8.5	-8.6	2.4	2.7	1.7	-0.3	3.3	5.1	5.4	n.a.	n.a.
Argentina												
Consolidated public sector	-7.4	-17.8	-18.7	-21.3	-18.5	-8.8	-6.4	-10.1	-10.0	-10.5	-6.1	-2.2
Financial public sector (quasifiscal)[4]	0.6	-1.1	-2.6	-3.4	-5.4	-3.4	-2.0	-3.4	-1.4	-5.8	-1.0	-8.0
Nonfinancial public sector	-8.0	-16.7	-18.1	-17.9	-13.1	-5.4	-4.4	-6.7	-8.6	-4.7	-5.1	-1.6
Interest payments	3.4	9.7	10.4	6.0	4.9	5.4	3.9	3.5	2.8	3.3	3.1	2.1
Primary	-4.6	-7.0	-5.7	-11.9	-8.2	0.0	-0.5	-3.2	-5.8	-1.4	-2.0	0.4

n.a. = not available.
[1] The figures for 1990 are preliminary.
[2] The figures for 1989 are preliminary.
[3] Includes Banco de México, nationalized commercial banks (as of September 1982), and the development bank.
[4] 1980–1986: corresponds to the quasifiscal deficit calculated by ECLAC (1991). 1987–1991: calculated using IMF and World Bank figures.

Source: Case studies.

Table 1.3. Public Debt Interest Payments
(Percentages of GDP)

	1980	Maximum in the decade	(Year)	1989
Mexico	3.5	19.7	(1987)	13.0
Argentina	3.4	10.4	(1982)	3.3
Costa Rica	5.0	6.8	(1983)	6.3[b]
Brazil	2.0	6.3	(1984/85)	6.3[b]
Peru	4.7	5.9	(1983/85)	1.7
Venezuela	3.5	5.4	(1984)	3.8
Ecuador	3.1	4.7	(1983/85)	3.9[a]
Colombia	1.5	4.5	(1987)	3.9
Uruguay	0.5	4.0	(1984)	2.5[a]
Chile	0.8	3.2	(1985)	2.2[b]
Bolivia	2.6	2.6	(1980)	2.0[a]

[a] Figure for 1987
[b] Figure for 1988.
Sources: *1990 Economic Survey of Latin America and the Caribbean,* ECLAC. Case Studies.

The size of the external public debt at the start of the decade, the way that private external debt ended up affecting public sector finances (through its absorption by the government or the central bank or through granting subsidies to service it), the rise of international interest rates, the suspension of external commercial bank credit following the debt crisis and, in some countries, the inordinate growth of the domestic indebtedness of the government and the central bank during the crisis, had an enormous impact on public finances in the 1980s. The interest payments on public debt exceeded 4 percent of GDP in some years in nearly all the countries of the region, reaching levels as high as 10.4 percent in Argentina in 1982 and even 19.7 percent in Mexico in 1987 (Table 1.3).

Changes in the international prices of commodities also caused great shocks in the public finances of various countries. Thus, for example, the operating surplus of PEMEX shrank by 7.2 percent of GDP between 1983 and 1989.[1] In Colombia, the deterioration of the finances of the National Coffee Fund (FNC) and of the taxes on coffee exports equaled 1.7 percent of GDP between 1979 and 1983 and 3.4 percent of GDP between 1986 and 1991. In Chile, the fall of copper prices in 1981 caused a decrease in the taxes on copper companies and in the operating surpluses of state enterprises, exceeding 2 percent of GDP.

A disaggregation exercise included in studies sponsored by ECLAC provides an estimate of the direct fiscal impact of the external variables (international interest rates and the prices of major export and import products), which

---

[1]This decrease began in 1984. Until 1983, the volume of Mexican oil exports was growing.

was on the order of 4.6 percent of GDP in Colombia in 1981 (2.8 percent in 1987), 3.7 percent in Chile in 1981, and 4.3 percent in Mexico in 1986 (Table 1.4).[2]

The financial crisis that erupted in most of the countries of the region in 1981 and the debt crisis in 1982 caused enormous increases in the quasifiscal deficit and in transfers and subsidies from the public sector to the private sector. In some countries, the quasifiscal deficits remained at high levels and even grew in the second half of the decade as a result of the domestic financing of consolidated deficits.

In Mexico, the deficit of the financial public sector was over 3 percent of GDP in 1983 and soared to 7.5 percent of GDP in 1987; in Argentina it rose to 2.6 percent of GDP in 1982, to 5.4 percent in 1984 and to 5.8 percent in 1989; and in Chile it exceeded 5 percent of GDP as an annual average from 1982 to 1985 (Table 1.2). Moreover, in all of these countries, the quasifiscal deficit was financed with monetary resources or central bank debt issues. In contrast, the quasifiscal deficit in Colombia was 1 percent or less of GDP in every year of the decade and was financed primarily with specifically earmarked taxes.[3] Budgetary transfers and subsidies to the private sector increased 4.1 percent of GDP in Chile between 1980 and 1984.

The domestic economic crisis caused by the concurrence of external shocks and the initial macroeconomic disequilibria, and in some cases by the adjustment programs themselves, had other effects on public finances. In particular, the acceleration of inflationary trends eroded the current revenue of the public sector in a number of ways:

• The well-known Oliveira-Tanzi effect, which is due to the delay between the establishment and the actual collection of taxes.
• The lags in the adjustment of public sector prices and rates, especially in cases where the latter were controlled as part of an anti-inflationary strategy.
• The contraction of the direct tax base caused by larger deductions for nominal interest payments,[4] the smaller real value of assets declared at historic prices, and other factors,[5] when there were no adjustments for inflation.
• The greater difficulty of control, which in some countries encouraged evasion. The control problem was accentuated in some countries where the fiscal crisis and the ensuing adjustments led to the contraction of real wages and a decline in the functional capacity of the tax administration.

---

[2]The figures for Chile, Colombia, and Mexico are not the same as those presented in the respective ECLAC studies due to classification differences.
[3]The part of the tax on coffee exports that went to the government.
[4]This factor largely explains the decrease in profit tax receipts in Mexico between 1982 and 1987, when the system of adjustment for inflation was introduced.
[5]In Argentina, for example, the improper indexation of accrued losses during the years of the crisis became an important source of contraction in the profit tax base until 1990.

Table 1.4. Determinants of the Change in the Fiscal Balance
(Contribution as a percentage of GDP)

	Periods of crisis					Periods of adjustment					
	Chile	Colombia	Mexico		Argentina	Chile	Colombia		Mexico		Argentina
	82–80	83–79	82–80	86–85	83–80	85–82	86–84	88–83	85–82	89–86	86–83
External variables	-1.7	-3.0	-0.2	-3.4	1.2	1.3	1.8	-1.9	-0.0	0.1	1.1
Real exchange rate	-2.4	-0.3	1.3	1.1	-3.2	7.1	1.2	0.8	1.3	-1.0	1.1
Domestic interest rate	0.2	-0.6	-2.3	-3.1	-8.1	-0.5	0.1	0.2	-2.4	7.8	-0.0
Other internal variables	-4.0	2.7	4.4	-1.9	-2.4	-0.7	1.4	2.4	-0.3	3.9	0.1
Fiscal policy variables	1.2	-9.2	-5.2	-0.6	3.7	-2.4	1.0	-0.1	5.6	0.8	4.0
Greater revenues	2.0	1.5	0.3	1.0	2.2	-1.6	1.7	2.7	2.2	-0.3	1.6
Greater expenditures	0.8	10.7	5.6	1.6	-1.5	0.8	0.7	2.8	-3.4	-1.1	-2.5
Explained variation	-6.7	-10.3	-2.1	-7.9	-8.9	4.9	5.5	1.4	4.2	11.6	6.3
Real variation	-9.3	-5.3	-6.7	-10.1	-13.9	-1.0	7.1	5.2	2.8	15.6	14.9

Sources: Fiscal Policy Series, ECLAC (various issues). Author's calculations.

- The growth of quasifiscal deficits due to the increase in the nominal interest rates paid by the central bank on its debt.[6]

The flight of capital that occurred in most Latin American countries as a result of the recession, economic instability, and expectations of devaluation, higher taxes, or an explicit or implicit repudiation of domestic debt, as well as the attractiveness of high international interest rates, especially in the United States, further eroded the tax base and encouraged even more evasion.

The recession had a negative effect on the fiscal balance because the income elasticity of taxes tends to be greater than that of expenditures. Moreover, in times of crisis, certain public expenditures such as unemployment and welfare benefits tend to increase.

The fact that nearly all the countries cut back on imports in order to generate a trade surplus large enough to permit the financing of external interest payments affected import tax receipts and the VAT from customs.

Real devaluation, carried out for the same purpose of generating trade surpluses or brought about by exchange runs, had different net effects on the balance of public finances, depending on whether or not the nonfinancial public sector was a net exporter of goods and services. Thus, it had positive—and very significant—net effects in Bolivia, Chile, Colombia, Ecuador, Mexico, and Venezuela and very negative effects in Argentina, Brazil, and other countries.

By way of example, real devaluation contributed the equivalent of 3.2 percent of GDP to the deterioration of the fiscal balance in Argentina in 1980–83, and 7.1 percent of GDP to the improvement in Chilean public finances between 1982 and 1985 (Tables 1.4 and 1.5). These figures are not corrected for the inflationary component of the external interest payment; thus, they exaggerate the adverse effects of devaluation on the fiscal deficit. Even so, taking into account the fact that during much of the decade the public sector in these countries had to make net financial transfers abroad, the impact of devaluation on the domestic financing requirements of the fiscal deficit was more negative than the above figures suggest.

Table 1.5 shows that in Chile, Colombia, and Mexico, the most significant fiscal effects of real devaluation occurred via its impact on public revenue from commodities exports (the operating surpluses of decentralized companies or entities and taxes and royalties) and, to a lesser extent, on the taxes on foreign trade, the VAT on imports,[7] external interest payments and public sector acquisitions abroad.

Finally, the rise of real interest rates in certain periods of the 1980s due to the

---

[6]This problem was especially acute in Argentina. See the section in Chapter Two entitled "Consequences of a Prolonged Fiscal Deficit: Overindebtedness."

[7]This latter component has become increasingly significant in various countries as the rate of the VAT increases and tariffs decrease (see Chapter Two).

Table 1.5. Contribution of the Exchange Rate to the Nonfinancial Public Sector Surplus (Deficit)
(Percentage of GDP)

	Chile		Colombia		Mexico				Argentina		
	81–78	85–81	84–80	88–84	83–81	84–83	86–84	89–86	80–77	83–80	87–83
I. Increase in revenues	-3.9	12.2	-0.4	3.6	6.8	-2.6	2.5	-2.6	-0.2	1.1	-0.1
A. Taxes on foreign trade	-1.0	1.7	-0.1	0.4	0.8	-0.1	0.2	-0.3	-1.4	1.6	-0.5
1. Imports	-1.0	1.7	-0.0	0.4	0.8	0.1	0.2	-0.3	-1.1	1.4	-0.2
2. Exports	—	—	-0.0	0.0	—	—	—	—	-0.3	0.2	-0.4
B. VAT on imports	-1.8	2.8	-0.1	0.5	0.5	-0.1	0.2	-0.3	n.a.	1.2	-0.1
C. Public enterprise surpluses	n.a.	7.0	-0.2	2.7	5.4	-2.4	2.1	-2.0	1.3	-1.7	0.6
D. Direct	-1.1	0.7	n.a.	n.a.	—	—	—	—	—	—	—
II. Increase in expenditures	-2.0	3.2	0.1	2.1	2.2	-1.0	1.0	-1.6	-2.7	4.4	-1.1
A. External debt interest	-0.7	1.6	0.0	0.4	2.2	-1.0	1.0	-1.6	-0.5	2.1	-0.8
B. Government purchases	-1.3	1.6	0.0	0.1	—	—	—	—	—	—	—
C. Investment	n.a.	n.a.	0.1	1.6	—	—	—	—	-2.2	2.2	-0.4
III. Surplus (deficit)	-1.9	9.0	-0.5	1.6	4.6	-1.6	1.5	-1.0	2.5	3.2	1.0

n.a. = not available
Sources: Fiscal Policy Series, ECLAC (various issues) and author's calculations.

anticipation of devaluation or debt repudiation or the application of contractive monetary policies, had considerable effect on public finances in countries that had accumulated a larger domestic public debt (i.e., debt of the government or of the central bank): Argentina (8 percent of GDP in 1980–83) and Mexico (2.3 percent of GDP in 1980–82 and 3.1 percent of GDP in 1985–86) (Table 1.4). For this purpose, it must be stressed once again that these figures, because they are not adjusted for the inflationary component of interest, over-estimate the effects on the fiscal deficit, although they do show the impact of higher interest rates on the additional gross financing requirements of the pub-lic sector.

The above notwithstanding, it has already been pointed out that the handling of the autonomous fiscal policy variables also had a negative effect at different times during the decade and in various countries of the region. In particular, the expansive nature of the fiscal policy explains, more than the external shocks and the behavior of other internal economic variables, the erosion of public finances in Colombia between 1979 and 1983, and in Mexico, especially in the 1980–82 period. In Argentina, the expansive fiscal policy of the 1977–80 period generated a large deficit (8 percent of GDP), which exacerbated the effect of the crisis in the early 1980s (Table 1.4 and the case studies).

Table 1.6 summarizes the contribution of the various revenue and expendi-ture items of the public sector balance to the deterioration of finances in the cri-sis periods. As can be seen, the above factors varied considerably in importance from one country to another.

Table 1.6. Dynamics of the Crisis
(Changes as percentages of GDP)

	Chile	Colombia	Mexico		Argentina
	80–84	79–83	80–82	85–86	80–83
Surplus (deficit)	−15.0	−8.6	−6.8	10.1	−13.7
Consolidated	−4.8	−0.8	3.1	3.0	−4.0
Quasifiscal	−10.2	−7.8	−9.9	−7.1	−9.7
Nonfinancial public sector	−8.6	−7.3	−5.2	−2.0	−7.1
Increase in revenues	−2.9	−1.4	0.9	−1.7	−4.7
Copper or oil	−0.7[a]	0.2	2.6	−2.6	—
Coffee	—	−1.3	—	—	—
Other current	3.3	0.3	−1.7	0.9	−4.6
Capital	1.1	—	—	—	−0.1
Increase in expenditures	7.3	6.4	10.8	5.4	5.0
Transfers to private sector	4.1	0.0	−0.6	0.1	1.7
Interest	1.6	0.5	4.7	5.1	2.6
Operating and investment	1.6	5.9	6.7	0.2	0.7

[a] Current revenue from copper is underestimated because no information is available concerning CODELCO operating surpluses.
Source: Case studies.

Table 1.7 Contribution of Tax Receipts to the Crisis
(Changes as percentages of GDP)

	Chile	Colombia	Mexico		Argentina
	80–84	79–83	80–82	85–86	80–83
Total	0.1	−2.0	−0.5	−1.9	−2.3
Copper or oil (direct and export)	−0.7	0.1	1.3	−2.4	0.0
Other direct (excl. copper and hydrocarbons)	−2.0	−0.7	−0.8	0.2	−1.6
VAT	−0.7	0.1	−0.5	−0.1	−0.7
Fuels and other specific products	2.7	0.1	−0.1	0.1	0.1
Foreign trade (excl. copper and hydrocarbons)	1.3	−0.8	−0.2	0.2	−0.9
Other national	−0.5	−0.8	−0.3	0.0	−1.0
Other territorial entities	0.0	0.4	0.0	0.0	n.a.

n.a. = not available
Source: Case studies.

The growth of the quasifiscal deficit was responsible for much of the deterioration of the consolidated balance in Argentina (1980–83), Chile (1980–84), and Mexico (1986). Such was not the case in Colombia (1979–83) or in Mexico in 1980–82, where, on the contrary, the central bank contributed net resources to cover part of the nonfinancial public sector deficit.

Meanwhile, in all cases, the growth of the nonfinancial public sector deficit was caused chiefly by increases in overall expenditures. In the majority of cases, most of the increase in expenditures was due to larger transfers and subsidies to the private sector as a result of the crisis and higher interest payments. The latter item was particularly significant in Argentina and Mexico. In Colombia, the increases in public investment explain most of the growth of expenditures. Larger operating and investment expenses also explain much of the increase in expenditures in Mexico in 1980–82.

The contraction of revenue from raw materials was significant in Chile in 1980–84,[8] in Colombia in 1979–83 and in Mexico in 1985–86. However, such was not the case in Mexico in 1980–82, when, despite the fall of oil prices, the growth of exports generated an increase in PEMEX surpluses.

In Argentina in 1980–83, an enormous decline in current revenue occurred, related both to the lag of public sector prices and rates and to the erosion of the base of direct taxes and the VAT as a result of proliferating exemptions and the acceleration of the inflationary trend. Current revenue not related to raw materials also shrank in Chile in 1980–84, in Mexico in 1980–82, and in Colombia in 1979–83, and increased slightly in Mexico in 1985–86 (Table 1.7).

The decrease (or slight increase) in current revenue not related to raw materials and the rise in total operating and investment expenses during periods of

---

[8]The figures in Table 1.6 underestimate this effect in Chile because they do not include the impact of the fall of copper prices on the operating surpluses of the copper companies.

Table 1.8. The Dynamics of Adjustment
(Changes as percentages of GDP)

	Chile	Colombia		Mexico		Argentina		
	84–89	83–86	83–89	82–85	86–89	83–86	83–90	90–91
Surplus (deficit)								
Consolidated	14.8	8.2	5.1	2.9	15.6	14.6	9.0	4.8
Quasifiscal[1]	4.8	−0.1	1.0	−4.2	6.3	1.4	0.1	0.4
Nonfinancial public sector	10.0	8.2	5.1	7.0	9.2	13.2	8.9	4.4
Primary	9.8	9.3	6.7	10.3	5.7	11.1	6.2	3.4
Increase in revenues	−0.0	7.0	5.1	0.6	2.2	6.2	−1.6	4.2
Copper or oil	5.8[a]	1.3	2.5	1.1	−1.4	—	—	—
Coffee	—	3.5	0.1	—	—	—	—	—
Other current	−5.6	2.3	2.6	−0.6	3.6	5.3	−1.6	2.7
Capital	−0.2	—	—	—	—	0.9	0.0	1.5
Increase in expenditures	−10.0	−1.2	0.1	−6.5	−7.0	−7.0	−10.5	−0.2
Transfers to private sector	−2.9	0.0	0.0	−1.0	−0.4	−1.1	−1.4	1.4
Interest	−0.2	1.1	1.7	3.3	−3.5	−2.1	−2.7	−1.0
Operating and investment	−6.9	−2.3	−1.6	−8.8	−3.1	−3.8	−6.4	0.6

[1]The quasifiscal deficit is assumed to be zero in Chile and Colombia in 1989, due to the fact that no information is available and in the previous year it had been reduced considerably (0.6 percent of GDP in Chile and 0.8 percent of GDP in Colombia).
[a]Current revenue from copper is underestimated because no information is available concerning CODELCO operating surpluses.
Source: Case studies.

crisis in all of the countries studied suggest the inability of fiscal policy to react opportunely to disequilibria caused by external or internal shocks. This inability is due both to the delay between the time when decisions are made and the time when their implementation actually reduces expenditures or increases revenue, and, in some cases, to the effort to apply an anticyclical fiscal policy (Colombia in 1979–84) or the slowness of the decision-making process itself.

The Adjustment

The governments responded more or less decisively and promptly to this process of erosion of the fiscal accounts, motivated both by the growing difficulty of financing the fiscal deficits (internal and external)[9] and by the growing

---

[9]The debit crisis blocked access to net external credit from commercial banks, except for modest amounts loaned to Chile and Colombia. Some countries, such as Colombia, nevertheless managed to maintain net positive flows for some years, thanks to the support of official banking. In such cases, the process of external and fiscal adjustment was postponed for a time. The greater relative access of Chile and Colombia to external credit, as compared to Argentina and Mexico, was due to the fact that they did not declare moratoriums on external payments and, in the case of Colombia, did not even renogotiate the debt.

conviction that it would not be possible to control the inflationary trends and the external disequilibria without taking action on this front (see Chapter Two).

In the periods of adjustment, reduction of the disequilibria in the fiscal accounts was accomplished primarily by reducing the quasifiscal deficit and overall spending, except in the case of Colombia, where the increase in revenue was largely responsible for the adjustment (Table 1.8). Spending cuts were made in those items that had increased as a result of the crisis (transfers and subsidies to the private sector and interest payments), as well as in operating and public investment expenses. The latter fell 5.7 percent of GDP in Chile in 1984–89, 4.5 percent in Argentina in 1983–91, 3 percent in Mexico in 1982–85 and 1.4 percent in 1986–89, and 1.9 percent in Colombia in 1983–90.

As in the periods of crisis, a substantial percentage of the contribution of increased revenue to the adjustment in Chile, Colombia, and Mexico was due to the improvement in revenue from the tapping of raw materials.

In Chile, the increase in revenue from copper (5.8 percent of GDP), especially from 1987, made it possible to offset a substantial reduction (5.9 percent of GDP) in other current revenues during the adjustment period. The improvement in the finances of the National Coffee Fund (FNC), due to the coffee boom of 1986, and the increased revenue generated by the surge in oil and mining exports in the first half of the decade explain nearly 60 percent of the fiscal adjustment in Colombia between 1983 and 1986. Subsequently, a coffee crisis erupted, wiping out earlier gains in that sector, and although oil and mining revenues kept increasing, other current revenues were increasing faster (especially from 1990). In Mexico during the 1982–85 period of adjustment, current revenue excluding oil decreased 0.6 percent of GDP. In contrast, in the 1986–89 period, they increased 3.6 percent of GDP.

In Argentina, the remarkable increase in current revenue in the 1983–86 period (5.3 percent of GDP) could not be sustained subsequently, and despite adjustments at the end of the decade, the increase in tax receipts from 0.4 percent of GDP between 1983 and 1991 was supplemented by a larger increase in temporary capital inflows from the privatization program.

The above figures suggest that the initial adjustment was achieved with little or no contribution from current revenue other than the earnings from commodities exports.

Considering the trend of tax receipts not derived from commodities exports, this tendency is even more pronounced. Table 1.9 shows the very slight, and

---

Domestic financing, in turn, became increasingly difficult because of its effects on domestic interest rates, the fragility of the financial system, the potential crowding-out of private investment and, in countries with larger domestic debt and high rates of inflation, because of debt repudiation expectations and the degree of demonetization of the economy. For more information, see the sections in Chapter Two entitled "Indexation and Inflationary Inertia" and "Consequences of a Prolonged Fiscal Deficit: Overindebtedness."

Table 1.9. Contribution of Tax Receipts to the Adjustment
(Changes as percentages of GDP)

	Chile	Colombia		Mexico		Argentina		
	84–89	83–86	83–89	82–85	86–89	83–86	83–90	90–91
Total	3.3	1.3	1.5	1.4	1.6	1.7	–0.9	5.0
Copper or oil (direct and export)	5.6	0.0	0.4	1.6	–0.1	0.0	–0.8	0.1
Other direct (except copper and hydrocarbons)	–0.3	–0.2	0.0	–0.7	1.3	1.3	–0.9	2.3
VAT	–1.3	0.6	0.8	0.6	0.3	–0.2	–2.2	1.9
Fuel and other specific products	–0.9	–0.1	–0.1	0.1	0.1	0.4	–0.2	–0.6
Foreign trade (except copper and hydrocarbons)	0.0	0.8	0.7	–0.2	–0.1	0.1	1.3	–0.5
Other national	–0.0	0.2	–0.2	–0.0	0.1	0.1	n.a.	n.a.
Other territorial entities	0.0	0.0	0.1	0.0	0.0	0.0	n.a.	n.a.

n.a. = not available.
Source: Case studies.

in some cases negative, contribution of increases in domestic tax receipts of a general nature (income tax and VAT) to the process of fiscal adjustment, especially in its initial phase. All of the countries started by raising the taxes on foreign trade (Argentina from 1983 to 1987; Chile, especially between 1984 and 1987; and Colombia between 1985 and 1988), and fuels, and a variety of minor taxes, before proceeding to increase basic taxes. This initial response was a result both of the fact that raising these taxes was politically less controversial than increasing the VAT or income taxes, and the fact that they respond more rapidly and with less administrative effort (which explains the name "tax handles"). Nevertheless, in most cases, these taxes had to be lowered again because of their negative effects on the allocation of resources in the economy.

In all cases, moreover, a considerable portion of the initial increase in revenue was a consequence of the exchange adjustment needed to restore external equilibrium or undertaken to bolster the effects of trade liberalization[10] (Tables 1.4 and 1.5).

Table 1.4 presents a summary of the results of ECLAC's disaggregation exercise for part of the adjustment period. The table clearly illustrates the fundamental role of the exchange adjustment in the initial fiscal adjustment process in Chile (1982–85). In fact, devaluation and the performance of the external variables account for all of the improvement in the fiscal balance in this period, since the effect of the autonomous fiscal policy variables and other internal variables was negative. The exchange adjustment also contributed significantly to the fiscal adjustment in Colombia in 1984–86 and in Mexico in 1982-85.

---

[10]In Chapter Two see the section on indexation and inflationary inertia. As mentioned above, in Argentina the net effects of devaluation on public finances was negative.

The table also shows that lowering the domestic real interest rate was a basic factor in the fiscal adjustment in Mexico in 1986-89, given the extreme weight of domestic interest payments.[11] This effect was even greater from 1989 when alleviation of the domestic and external public debt burden made the convergence of domestic and external interest rates possible (see Oks, 1992).

Finally, the inflow of capital from privatization also played an important role in the adjustment of the fiscal accounts in Chile in 1984-88 and in Mexico and Argentina in the late 1980s and early 1990s.

It was only in the late 1980s or early 1990s that a process of intensifying the collection of VAT and income taxes was initiated in all of the countries studied. There appear to be several reasons for this:

• The growing perception that additional cuts in public spending (specifically on physical infrastructure and investment in human capital) could compromise the success of the liberalization process and future economic growth.
• The growing conviction that the fiscal adjustment should be permanent and, therefore, that it was right to reinforce basic taxes and not depend so much on booms in commodities, tax handles, the proceeds from privatization, nor on the beneficial fiscal effects of devaluation (in countries where its impact on the fiscal deficit is positive), since all of these effects are clearly temporary.

Summary

The results of the fiscal crises and adjustments that occurred during the decade, as well as the fiscal impact of the structural reforms (Chapter Three), set in motion medium-term trends with both similarities and differences in the various countries studied (Tables 1.10 and 1.11). Following is a summary, first of national experiences and then of the common trends.

National Experiences

Chile.   The decade began with a sizable fiscal surplus (5.6 percent of GDP), which resulted from the enormous bolstering of public finances that took place after the serious deficit incurred during the Unidad Popular period. In 1980, current revenues were greater by 15 percent of GDP than in 1973 and equaled the 1970 figure, not counting the taxes on copper companies. Tax receipts registered an increase of 2.2 percent of GDP in the 1970s, concentrated primarily

---

[11]For more information on this subject, see Chapter Three.

in income tax and the VAT. In 1975, the most ambitious and advanced tax reform in the hemisphere was introduced.

In 1980, total public expenditures, on the other hand, were 9.7 percent of GDP less than in 1970, owing both to austerity policies and the long-term objective of reducing the size of government.

In the 1980s, the tendency to reduce overall public spending continued (which, in 1990, was 3.8 percent of GDP less than in 1980), but unlike the previous decade, public finances deteriorated. This was reflected both by the overall decrease in current revenues (8.9 percent of GDP between 1980 and 1989, excluding copper receipts and capital earnings) and by the change in composition of the structure of revenues and the existence of substantial fiscal and quasifiscal deficits between 1982 and 1985, the net result of which was a substantial rise in public indebtedness.

The change in the composition of public revenues during the last decade was the reverse of what might be expected in a process of liberalization and modernization: there were decreases in income tax (-2.3 percent of GDP) and the VAT (-2 percent of GDP), in social security contributions (-3.7 percent of GDP) and in nontax revenues (-3.5 percent of GDP). These decreases were the result of the 1984 tax reform (which lowered direct taxes), the reduction of the rate of the VAT in 1987, the social insurance reform[12] in the early 1980s and the privatization of public enterprises which were generating substantial operating surpluses.

The deterioration of the structure of current revenues was partly offset by an enormous increase in the taxation of copper (equal to 5.1 percent of GDP) and foreign trade (1.3 percent of GDP), by a reduction in current expenditures (of 2.4 percent of GDP) based on the contraction of wages and salaries (-4.6 percent of GDP) and, temporarily, by larger capital inflows from the privatization program (the value of the sales of public enterprises rose from 1.9 percent to 3 percent of GDP per year between 1986 and 1989 and about 1 percent in 1990).

In other words, the dwindling of domestic revenues was partly offset by the fiscal effect of real devaluation,[13] the positive trend of international copper prices, the return to higher taxes on international trade, the decrease in the size of the central government payroll and the sale of assets.

The tax reform of 1990 constituted a change in direction with respect to the orientation of the fiscal management of the decade. Given the upward pressure

---

[12]It has been estimated that the social insurance reform caused a cash deficit in the consolidated public finances of approximately 5 percent of GDP for more than 12 years (Ortuzar, 1986). This public deficit had as its counterpart an increase in private saving through the new pension funds. In fact, these funds had to be used to finance some of the public shortfalls caused by the reform. Although this obligatory investment of the funds facilitated public financing in the years when there was a consolidated deficit, it generated a growing government debt toward the funds, imposing a restraint on future public financing.

[13]As indicated above, this explains most of the initial adjustment.

Table 1.10. Trend of the Public Sector in the 1970s and 1980s
(Change as a percentage of GDP)

	Chile[1]			Colombia[2]			Mexico[3]		Argentina		
	80–70	89–80	90–82	80–70	89–80	91–89	80–72	89–80	80–74	90–80	91–90
Surplus (deficit)											
Consolidated	n.a.	−0.2	n.a.	n.a.	−0.6	n.a.	n.a.	1.6	n.a.	0.4	3.9
Quasifiscal	n.a.	0.0	n.a.	n.a.	−1.0	n.a.	n.a.	2.3	n.a.	−2.0	0.4
Nonfinancial public sector	12.2	−0.2	−2.9	−1.1	0.5	1.8	1.2	−0.7	1.6	2.4	3.5
Primary	12.6	1.2	−2.8	−0.8	2.9	1.7	2.1	8.8	4.6	2.2	2.5
Increase in revenues	2.6	−2.9	−3.0	−0.2	5.3	—	6.7	1.9	2.5	−3.2	3.3
Copper or oil	−1.2	5.1	−2.5	−0.8	2.7	3.1	3.1	1.7	—	—	—
Coffee	—	—	—	n.a.	−0.9	—	—	—	—	—	—
Other current	−0.1	−8.9	−0.5	0.4	3.6	3.7	3.7	0.3	2.5	4.1	1.8
Capital	3.8	0.9	—	—	—	—	—	—	0.1	0.9	1.5
Increase in expenditures	−9.7	−2.7	−1.0	0.9	4.9	−1.3	5.5	2.7	0.9	−5.6	−0.2
Transfers to the private sector	0.7	1.2	−0.4	0.0	0.0	0.0	2.0	−1.9	−1.5	−0.4	1.4
Interest	0.4	1.4	0.1	0.4	2.4	−0.2	0.9	9.5	3.0	−0.2	−1.0
Operating	−5.6	−5.0	0.1	−0.6	1.2	−1.0	0.5	−0.3	−0.4	−1.2	−0.3
Investment	−5.2	−0.3	−0.8	1.2	1.3	−0.1	2.2	4.7	−1.2	−3.8	−0.3

n.a. = not available.
[1] The data for 1990 are provisional.
[2] The data for 1991 are provisional.
[3] The figures for Mexico are for the central government because data for the nonfinancial public sector are unavailable.
Source: Case studies.

Table 1.11. Trend of Tax Receipts in the 1970s and 1980s
(Change as a percentage of GDP)

	Chile[1]			Colombia[2]			Mexico[3]		Argentina		
	80–70	89–80	90–82	80–70	89–80	91–89	80–72	89–80	80–74	90–80	91–90
Total	2.2	3.4	-2.0	-1.3	2.2	0.2[3]	6.3	1.3[4]	2.8	-3.0[4]	3.2
Direct	-0.4	2.8	-3.3	-1.3	0.6	1.6	4.9	-0.0	0.1	-1.5	0.1
Copper or oil	-1.2	5.1	-2.5	-0.0	0.6	n.a.	3.0	0.4	—	—	—
Others	0.8	-2.3	-0.8	-1.3	0.1	n.a.	1.9	-0.4	0.1	-1.5	0.1
Indirect	2.4	0.0	0.9	1.0	0.7	0.3	0.8	1.8	2.8	-2.2	4.2
VAT	n.a.	-2.0	0.7	0.9	0.7	0.3	1.5	0.4	2.5	-1.8	2.3
Fuel and other specific products	n.a.	0.6	0.2	0.1	-0.0	0.0	-0.8	1.5	0.3	-0.4	1.9
Foreign trade	0.3	1.3	-0.5	-0.0	0.3	-0.5	-0.1	-0.3	0.1	0.3	-0.6
Other national	0.0	0.7	0.0	-0.3	-0.1	-0.0	0.7	-0.2	-0.2	0.4	0.5
Other territorial entities	n.a.	n.a.	n.a.	-0.7	0.3	n.a.	n.a.	n.a.	n.a.	n.a.	n.a.

n.a. = not available
[1] The data for 1990 are provisional.
[2] The data for 1991 are provisional.
[3] Other territorial entities not included in the final period.
[4] Other territorial entities not included in any period.
Source: Case studies.

on the real exchange rate generated by the inflow of external capital, the fall of copper prices and the uncertainty about their future trend, as well as the need to increase social and infrastructure spending, the focus was again on raising domestic taxes (income and VAT).

Mexico. Mexican public finances in the last two decades can be divided into two distinct phases with very different trends. Between 1972 and 1982, government spending increased excessively, especially beginning in 1980 (between 1980 and 1982, aggregate spending increased 10.8 percent of GDP and the consolidated deficit of the nonfinancial public sector increased 9 percent of GDP), supported by tax receipts and the extraordinary borrowing power afforded by the oil discoveries of the late 1970s, the high international price of crude oil and the permissiveness of the external financial markets. In contrast, starting in 1982 there was an appreciable fiscal adjustment (the consolidated balance of the nonfinancial public sector improved 10.1 percent of GDP between 1982 and 1989, and even more in the following years) as a result of the two external shocks that so greatly affected public finances and the Mexican economy: the debt crisis of 1982 and the fall of international oil prices, especially from 1986.

The upsurge in public expenditures (other than interest payments) that occurred between 1972 and 1982 was reversed entirely in the following years. The most remarkable change in the fiscal balance of the central government in the two decades (1972-1989) was, therefore, the large increase in interest payments on public debt (10.4 percent of GDP), necessitated by the accumulation of domestic debt to finance the large deficits of the 1980s, and its partial compensation through a rise in current revenues (8.6 percent of GDP). The latter, in turn, was largely due to increases in direct and indirect taxes on petroleum and natural gas (4.8 percent of GDP).

The consolidated balance in the 1980s indicates a significant decline in public investment (4.7 percent of GDP). Much of this decrease was due to smaller PEMEX investments (2 percent of GDP), owing both to the erosion of its gross operating surpluses and the fact that, despite the fall of international prices, the government kept its tax receipts from oil at a constant level, by increasing the taxes on the extraction of hydrocarbons for domestic sale in 1983 as well as the taxes on the domestic sale of gasoline. The other public enterprises improved their balances during the decade, thanks to the effort to raise the real prices and rates of the goods and services they produce.

Most of the increases in non-petroleum taxes between 1972 and 1989 (4 percent of GDP in all, of which income tax represented 1.5 percent of GDP and VAT 1.9 percent of GDP) occurred in the 1970s. Between 1980 and 1989 they increased a scant 0.3 percent of GDP. Income tax receipts in 1987 were 1.8 percent of GDP below the figure for 1980, and in 1989 hardly reached that level. The slight increase in VAT receipts during the decade (0.4 percent of GDP) consisted entirely of import tax receipts, due to the effects of devaluation. The decrease in broad-based domestic taxes (VAT and income tax) was reversed from 1988 and, more particularly, from 1990, when the growth of receipts more than compensated for the negative effects of the revaluation of the peso and the customs rebate on total tax receipts. Also contributing to this was a series of legal reforms starting in 1987 and some substantial administrative changes, especially with respect to the VAT (Chapter Five).

Argentina.   The trend of Argentina's public finances was highly erratic in the last two decades. The substantial decline in the first half of the 1970s was followed by a partial adjustment in 1976 and 1977, another decline from 1978 to 1983 and an adjustment effort from 1984. This effort suffered a setback in 1987–89, but fiscal equilibrium was finally achieved in 1991–92.

The net fiscal position of the last decade (1980–90) was characterized by a reduction of 5.6 percent of GDP in total expenditures (especially in public investment: 3.8 percent of GDP) and a significant drop in tax receipts (-3.2 percent of GDP), especially income tax (-1.5 percent of GDP) and the VAT (-1.8 percent). Social security contributions also decreased (-1 percent of GDP). Conversely, from 1991, current revenues improved significantly (3.3 percent of GDP) as a result of increases in the collection of VAT (2.3 percent of GDP), other consumption taxes (1.9 percent of GDP) and social security contributions.

Direct taxes deteriorated throughout the last two decades: from barely 2.3 percent of GDP in 1970, a low figure compared to other countries with similar income levels, direct taxes fell to lows of 0.6 percent of GDP in 1984 and 1990. Receipts of the VAT (introduced in 1974) rose to 5.1 percent of GDP in 1981, fell to 1.7 percent in 1989 and then rallied sufficiently to reach 2.8 percent in 1990. The decrease in basic tax receipts in the 1980s was due to the combined effects of exemptions granted under the industrial promotion system, which became a major source of erosion of the tax base, legislative measures such as the reduction of the VAT in 1987, the acceleration of inflation and the demonetization of the economy, and a serious decline in the administration of taxes.

During the decade, however, other taxes were created or increased, the fiscal effect of which was temporary at best. Such was the case with export taxes (which climbed to 1.6 percent of GDP in 1989 and then fell to 0.12 percent in 1991), tariffs (which rose to 1.7 percent of GDP in 1987 and slipped to 0.3 percent in 1990 in the wake of trade liberalization), taxes on energy products (which amounted to 3.5 percent of GDP in 1985 and 1986, even though the net receipts[14] thereof were negative in various years and remained below 1 percent of GDP between 1985 and 1990) and a large number of inefficient taxes

---

[14] That is, net of "offsets" and specific allocations benefiting the very companies in the sector.

(which ranged from a minimum of 0.7 percent of GDP in 1975 to a maximum of 2.7 percent in 1990), the most noteworthy being the taxes on financial and exchange transactions.

Late in the decade there was a steady upturn in VAT receipts (which rebounded to 5.1 percent of GDP in 1991) and direct taxes (receipts of which were on the rise in 1992), as a result of various legal and administrative changes.

Similarly, social security contributions after falling to 2.3 percent of GDP in 1982 and 1983 (from 5.4 percent in 1980) as a result of the recession, the erosion of real wages, and the social insurance reform introduced at the beginning of the decade , jumped to 6.2 percent of GDP in 1991.

Lastly, it should be pointed out that much of the deterioration in Argentina's fiscal balance was caused by provincial finances, which enjoy complete autonomy, and that the adjustment undertaken in 1983 was borne essentially by the national government and, to a lesser extent and with a slight delay, by the public enterprises. In 1987, provincial finances registered a deficit of more than twice that of 1977; and, despite the efforts of the central government to increase and regularize the transfer of resources and to block provincial access to sources of financing the deficit from that point forward, the deficit kept growing until the end of the decade (see the section in Chapter Four entitled "The Fiscal Impact of Decentralization").

Colombia.   Unlike the experience in other countries, in Colombia in the last two decades an upward trend was observed both in total expenses (4.5 percent of GDP from 1970 to 1991) and in the current revenue of the public sector (5.6 percent of GDP). Most of this growth occurred in 1980 and subsequent years (3.6 percent and 5.8 percent, respectively).

The growth of expenditures was mostly due to interest payments (2.6 percent of GDP) and capital expenditures (2.4 percent of GDP). The increase in revenues was chiefly the result of receipts from the oil industry (direct taxes, royalties and ECOPETROL surpluses, which, as a whole, expanded 2.57 percent of GDP between 1980 and 1989) and the large surpluses of other public enterprises.

Non-petroleum tax receipts, however, decreased slightly in the 1970s and early 1980s (until 1984), and then recovered. The steady rise in VAT receipts (1.6 percent of GDP in the two decades) made up for the slight decrease in the other categories.

As in other countries of the region, Colombia's fiscal adjustment effort (in the latter half of the 1980s) was concentrated at the national level of the public sector, while departmental and municipal expenditures and deficits grew uninterruptedly throughout the decade. This was partly the result of a deliberate policy to decentralize public spending. Unlike the experience in other countries, however, the adjustment originated more in the decentralized enterprises and entities at the national level than in the central administration.

In fact, between 1980 and 1985, the sizable increase in consolidated public investment was focused on the development of large energy and mining projects (from 2.3 percent to 4.6 percent of GDP), and its subsequent decline (from 4.6 percent to 1.9 percent of GDP in 1991) was a natural consequence of the culmination of those projects. As a result, during the adjustment period, other public investment rose from 3.7 percent of GDP in 1984 to 5.4 percent in 1991.

In other words, the "adjustment" of Colombian public spending, unlike that of other countries of the region, did not require significant sacrifices in social spending or "cuts" in public investment that could have affected economic growth rates. Moreover, the considerable public investment in oil and mining in the first half of the decade bore fruit in the second half, not only in terms of its contribution to the balance of payments but, above all, in fiscal terms. Much of the rise in the consolidated current revenue of the public sector was due to increases in royalties, petroleum taxes and the operating surpluses of state mining companies. Real devaluation of the peso also contributed to this result.

The fiscal effort, properly speaking, was thus limited to increasing the taxes on imports (which were 2.4 percent of GDP in 1987) and cutting expenditures and investments in other decentralized entities. The government's efforts were focused on establishing appropriate mechanisms to transfer surplus resources from the enterprises and the FNC to the national budget and to other entities, and on decreasing its transfers to public establishments so that it could finance growing transfers to the departments and municipalities as well as the central administration's own deficit.

Later, the fiscal consequences of the coffee crisis that followed the collapse of the International Coffee Agreement, the trade tax abatement and the appreciation of the peso in 1991 necessitated the reinforcement of non-petroleum direct taxes (receipts of which grew from 3.2 percent of GDP in 1988 to 4.5 percent in 1991 and will increase again with the reform of 1992) and the VAT (which climbed to 3.2 percent of GDP in 1991 and will increase again with the reform of 1992).

Common Trends

The summaries of national experiences in Chile, Mexico, Argentina and Colombia reveal the following common trends:

• In recent years, the countries studied have tended to cut public spending excluding interest payments—Chile since 1974, Argentina since 1980, Mexico since 1982, and Colombia since 1985—as a result both of the fiscal crisis in the 1980s and of the tendency to reduce the size of government.

• Comparing the level of spending in the late 1980s with the level in the early 1970s (excluding interest payments), a very considerable reduction can be observed in Argentina and Chile, a modest decrease in Mexico and a significant increase in Colombia. The latter two countries boosted their fiscal capacity with the revenue from their oil discoveries (Mexico in the late 1970s and Colombia in the 1980s).

• The current increased reliance on public finances (in those two countries and in Chile) with respect to earnings from commodities exports (in comparison with said earnings in the early 1970s), points to the necessity of creating mechanisms to stabilize fiscal expenditures (Chapter Three).

• In the 1970s, all of the countries increased their income and sales taxes, converting the latter to a value-added tax (Argentina, Chile, and Colombia[15] toward the middle of the decade and Mexico in 1980). In contrast, income tax receipts in the 1980s (excluding the taxes on copper and oil) decreased in all of them, and VAT receipts in some as a result of legislative measures enacted for structural and cyclical reasons (Chapter Five), the economic crisis and the decline in administrative capacity. The decrease in receipts of the value-added tax on domestic business activity was greater since the VAT on imports grew as a result of both real devaluation and trade liberalization.

• Faced with fiscal crises in the early 1980s, all of the countries reacted basically by cutting expenditures and, initially, by raising public sector prices and rates and taxes other than income and the value-added tax (on imports in Chile and Colombia, on energy products in Argentina and Mexico, and on exports and exchange and financial transactions in Argentina).

• The real devaluation carried out in the 1980s to generate the trade surplus necessary to finance larger external interest payments played a definitive role in the fiscal adjustment of Chile, Colombia and Mexico, countries in which the public sector is a net exporter of goods and services. This suggests that fiscal objectives also had a hand in the exchange adjustment in those countries and that the variability of exchange management in Argentina resulted partly from conflict with the fiscal goals (Chapter Two).

• Since the late 1980s or early 1990s, all of the countries have resumed increasing basic taxes (income tax and the VAT). This fact seems to be related to: (i) the growing conviction that a permanent and realistic fiscal adjustment is important for the equilibrium of an open economy (experience showed that the adjustment of other current revenues was essentially temporary and that further spending cuts undermined the objectives of competitiveness and growth), and (ii) the necessity of generating fiscal surpluses to offset the heavy inflow of capital observed since 1991 (see Chapter Two).

---

[15]Colombia, however, continued charging sales tax on manufactures and imports until 1983.

CHAPTER TWO

FISCAL ADJUSTMENT, STABILIZATION AND LIBERALIZATION

Overview

The experience of Latin America in the last two decades leaves little doubt as to the importance of the fiscal problem in stabilization programs, regardless of whether fiscal adjustment or equilibrium was necessary for the success of such programs (as in Chile and Colombia in the 1970s, in Mexico in the late 1980s, and in Argentina in 1991 and temporarily in 1985 and 1986) or whether the inadequacy of the adjustment had derailed the stabilization programs (as in Argentina from 1982 to 1985 and from 1987 to 1989, and in Mexico from 1982 to 1985).[16] Nevertheless, the relationship between fiscal equilibrium or adjustment and stabilization has not always been a close one.

In the early 1970s, there was a concurrent rise in the rate of inflation and an increase in the fiscal deficit in the four countries studied (Table 2.1). The acceleration of international inflation generated inflationary pressures, which were amplified in all of the countries by expansive fiscal policies and, in Colombia, by an active exchange policy that prevented appreciation of the peso (and even resulted in real depreciation), despite improvement in the terms of trade and the accumulation of international reserves.

---

[16] The same thing happened in Brazil.

Table 2.1. Macroeconomic Indicators

		1971	1972	1973	1974	1975	1976	1977	1978	1979
I.	**Chile**									
A.	Growth rates									
	1. Gross domestic product	9.0	-1.2	-5.6	1.0	-12.9	3.5	9.9	8.2	8.3
	2. Consumer price index									
	Year's average	20.0	74.8	361.5	504.7	374.7	211.8	81.9	40.1	33.4
	Year's end	19.4	149.2	558.6	376.0	340.7	174.3	63.4	30.3	36.9
	3. Nominal exchange rate									
	Year's average	3.2	57.1	468.7	650.8	480.3	165.8	64.9	47.0	17.7
	Year's end	29.2	56.2	1340.0	419.4	354.5	104.9	60.5	21.4	14.9
B.	Percentages of GDP									
	1. Current account surplus (deficit)	-1.9	-3.9	2.7	-2.6	-6.8	1.5	-4.1	-7.1	-5.7
	2. SPNF surplus (deficit)	-8.7	-15.3	-26.1	-30.5	-5.4	3.6	1.7	2.1	4.8
C.	Real exchange rate[1]									
	Year's average	54.7	50.8	66.5	91.6	124.3	112.1	102.5	115.8	113.7
	Year's end	70.8	46.5	110.5	135.3	149.4	117.0	122.7	124.6	116.8
II.	**Colombia**									
A.	Growth rates									
	1. Gross domestic product	6.0	7.7	6.7	5.7	2.3	4.7	4.2	8.5	5.4
	2. Consumer price index									
	Year's average	9.1	13.4	20.8	24.3	22.9	20.2	33.1	17.8	24.7
	Year's end	14.5	13.6	23.9	25.9	17.8	25.7	28.4	18.8	28.8
	3. Nominal exchange rate									
	Year's average	8.1	8.7	8.1	10.3	18.7	12.2	6.0	6.3	8.8
	Year's end	9.5	9.0	8.8	15.5	15.1	10.2	4.5	8.0	7.3
B.	Percentages of GDP									
	1. Current account surplus (deficit)	-5.8	-2.2	-0.5	-2.8	-1.3	1.1	1.9	1.1	1.8
	2. SPNF surplus (deficit)	-2.7	-2.7	-3.4	0.1	0.1	1.2	-1.2	0.8	0.3
C.	Real exchange rate									
	Year's average[1]	128.9	128.7	122.4	120.6	127.1	125.3	106.3	103.3	100.3
	Year's end[1]	128.9	125.9	120.2	123.8	129.4	119.0	103.4	102.6	96.8
	Year's end[2]	110.3	115.1	114.1	113.2	117.4	117.4	101.7	100.2	96.9

Table 2.1. (cont.)

	1980	1981	1982	1983	1984	1985	1986	1987	1988	1989	1990
I. Chile											
A. Growth rates											
1. Gross domestic product	7.8	5.5	-14.1	-0.7	6.4	2.5	5.6	5.7	7.4	10.0	2.2
2. Consumer price index											
Year's average	35.1	19.7	9.9	27.3	19.9	30.7	19.5	19.9	14.7	17.0	28.0
Year's end	31.2	9.5	20.7	23.1	23.0	26.4	17.4	21.5	12.7	21.4	27.3
3. Nominal exchange rate											
Year's average	4.7	0.0	30.5	54.9	25.1	63.3	19.8	13.7	11.6	9.0	14.2
Year's end	0.0	0.0	88.3	19.2	46.5	43.4	11.4	16.3	3.8	20.3	13.4
B. Percentages of GDP											
1. Current account surplus (deficit)	-7.1	-14.5	-9.5	-5.7	-11.0	-8.3	-6.9	-4.3	0.8	-3.0	-2.8
2. SPNF surplus (deficit)	5.8	0.7	-3.7	-2.8	-4.4	-2.5	-1.5	0.1	2.4	5.6	2.7
C. Real exchange rate[1]											
Year's average	100.0	92.2	118.2	145.9	158.9	205.6	210.0	206.7	208.3	204.4	195.1
Year's end	100.0	99.5	181.1	161.9	200.4	235.9	228.4	226.3	217.7	225.7	213.2
II. Colombia											
A. Growth rates											
1. Gross domestic product	4.1	2.3	0.9	1.6	3.4	3.1	5.8	5.4	3.7	3.6	4.2
2. Consumer price index											
Year's average	26.5	27.5	24.5	19.8	16.1	24.0	18.9	23.3	28.1	25.8	29.1
Year's end	25.9	28.3	24.1	16.6	18.3	22.5	20.9	24.0	28.2	26.1	32.4
3. Nominal exchange rate											
Year's average	11.1	15.2	17.8	23.0	27.9	41.2	36.5	24.9	23.3	27.9	31.3
Year's end	15.7	16.0	19.0	26.3	28.3	51.2	27.2	20.4	27.4	29.2	31.1
B. Percentages of GDP											
1. Current account surplus (deficit)	-0.8	-5.4	-7.8	-7.8	-3.7	-5.2	1.1	0.9	-0.8	0.5	1.0
2. SPNF surplus (deficit)	-2.3	-5.5	-6.0	-7.4	-5.9	-4.4	-0.3	-1.9	-2.5	-2.4	-0.7
C. Real exchange rate											
Year's average[1]	100.0	99.7	100.0	106.0	121.7	143.5	167.8	178.3	176.5	188.1	201.5
Year's end[1]	100.0	100.0	99.7	112.0	126.3	161.8	172.1	174.4	181.0	194.1	203.9
Year's end[2]	100.0	95.8	90.3	87.4	84.8	112.6	144.5	149.0	153.3	164.8	188.0

Table 2.1. (cont.)

		1971	1972	1973	1974	1975	1976	1977	1978	1979
III.	**Mexico**									
A.	Growth rates									
	1. Gross domestic product	4.2	8.5	8.4	6.1	5.6	4.2	3.4	8.3	9.2
	2. Consumer price index									
	Year's average	5.3	5.0	12.0	23.8	15.2	15.6	29.0	17.5	18.2
	Year's end	5.0	5.7	21.3	20.6	11.3	27.2	20.7	16.2	20.0
	3. Nominal exchange rate									
	Year's average	0.0	0.0	-0.0	0.0	0.0	23.4	46.3	0.9	0.2
	Year's end	0.0	0.0	0.0	0.0	0.0	59.6	14.0	-0.1	0.3
B.	Percentages of GDP									
	1. Current account surplus (deficit)	-2.0	-1.9	-2.4	-3.7	-4.3	-3.6	-2.1	-2.9	-3.8
	2. SPNF surplus (deficit)[a,b]	n.a.	-0.5	-1.9	-1.7	-0.3	-1.1	-0.6	-0.4	-0.4
C.	Real exchange rate[1]									
	Year's average	117.5	115.6	109.6	96.4	93.2	105.0	126.9	117.3	110.6
	Year's end	122.4	119.8	107.4	100.0	96.1	126.4	127.4	119.5	113.2
IV.	**Argentina**									
A.	Growth rates									
	1. Gross domestic product	3.4	1.9	3.2	6.2	-0.7	-0.2	6.2	-3.3	7.3
	2. Consumer price index									
	Year's average	34.7	56.4	61.2	23.5	182.9	444.0	176.0	175.5	159.5
	Year's end	39.1	64.2	43.7	39.9	336.1	347.4	160.4	169.9	139.7
	3. Nominal exchange rate									
	Year's average	19.3	10.6	0.0	0.0	631.5	282.7	191.2	95.2	65.5
	Year's end	25.0	0.0	0.0	0.0	1117.7	350.8	117.7	67.9	81.3
B.	Percentages of GDP									
	1. Current account surplus (deficit)	-1.8	-0.9	1.8	0.2	-3.3	1.7	2.7	4.3	-1.0
	2. SPNF surplus (deficit)	n.a.	n.a.	n.a.	-9.3	-14.5	-10.4	-4.1	-5.8	-5.5
C.	Real exchange rate[1]									
	Year's average	232.6	167.7	110.5	99.3	280.3	208.5	234.3	178.7	126.8
	Year's end	243.3	153.2	116.0	93.1	278.1	293.7	262.2	177.9	135.6

Table 2.1. (cont.)

	1980	1981	1982	1983	1984	1985	1986	1987	1988	1989	1990
III. Mexico											
A. Growth rates											
1. Gross domestic product	8.3	7.9	-0.8	-5.3	3.7	2.7	-3.7	1.7	1.4	3.1	4.4
2. Consumer price index											
Year's average	26.4	27.9	58.9	101.8	85.5	57.7	86.2	131.8	114.2	20.0	26.7
Year's end	29.8	28.7	96.9	80.8	59.2	63.7	105.7	159.2	51.7	19.7	29.9
3. Nominal exchange rate											
Year's average	0.6	6.8	130.1	112.9	39.7	53.1	138.2	125.3	64.9	8.3	14.3
Year's end	2.0	12.8	267.8	49.2	33.8	93.0	148.5	139.3	3.2	15.8	11.5
B. Percentages of GDP											
1. Current account surplus (deficit)	-5.5	-6.4	-3.6	3.8	2.4	0.6	-1.3	2.8	-1.4	-1.9	-2.2
2. SPNF surplus (deficit)[a,b]	-6.9	-13.5	-16.8	-10.0	-9.2	-9.8	-16.9	-18.5	-11.6	-7.6	n.a.
C. Real exchange rate[1]											
Year's average	100.0	92.1	141.6	154.2	135.8	136.4	177.7	179.2	143.5	135.7	129.1
Year's end	100.0	95.5	183.4	157.1	137.3	168.0	205.1	197.7	140.5	142.2	129.5
IV. Argentina											
A. Growth rates											
1. Gross domestic product	1.5	-6.7	-5.0	2.9	2.5	-4.4	5.6	2.5	-2.5	-4.5	0.4
2. Consumer price index											
Year's average	100.8	104.5	164.8	343.6	626.7	672.1	90.1	131.3	342.9	3079.9	2314.0
Year's end	87.6	131.3	209.7	433.7	888.0	385.4	81.9	174.8	387.7	4924.0	1343.9
3. Nominal exchange rate											
Year's average	39.5	139.6	488.8	306.2	542.4	789.6	56.7	127.4	308.2	4736.7	1051.8
Year's end	23.1	263.8	569.8	379.2	868.4	347.9	57.0	198.3	256.5	13325.6	211.1
B. Percentages of GDP											
1. Current account surplus (deficit)	-8.4	-8.2	-4.1	-3.8	-3.2	-1.4	-3.6	-5.3	-1.7	-2.2	1.7
2. SPNF surplus (deficit)	-8.0	-18.7	-16.1	-17.9	-13.1	-5.4	-4.4	-8.7	-8.6	-4.7	-5.1
C. Real exchange rate[1]											
Year's average	100.0	129.3	305.2	266.3	265.9	317.2	266.4	271.6	260.3	415.1	208.8
Year's end	100.0	171.3	384.9	356.6	363.6	348.1	303.9	344.4	262.9	735.2	168.1

n.a. = not available
[1] Calculated using the exchange rate for the dollar. Base 1980 = 100.
[2] FEDESARROLLO calculations based on the price indices of the products with the largest share of Colombia's trade. Base 1980 = 100.
[a] The data for the 1972-79 period are for the central government since no data are available for the other levels of government.
[b] The figure for 1989 is provisional.
Sources: *International Financial Statistics*, IMF. Case studies.

Figure 2.1. Chile: External and Fiscal Surplus, 1971-90
(Percentage of GDP)

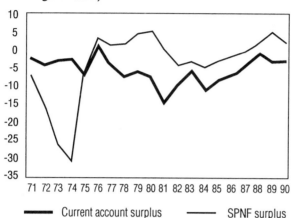

Subsequently, the balance of public finances and the inflation rate continued to move more or less in the same direction in Argentina and, in the 1980s, in Mexico. In both cases, however, acceleration of the inflationary trend was also related to massive nominal devaluations carried out in response to external shocks or triggered by exchange runs (Figures 2.3, 2.4a and b, 2.5 and 2.6).

In Chile and Colombia, the relationship between changes in the inflation rate and the fiscal deficit is less clear. The periods of greatest fiscal crisis, for example, did not coincide with accelerations of the inflationary trend (Colombia in 1979-83, Chile in 1982-85) and there were periods of mounting inflation in conditions of fiscal equilibrium (Colombia in 1976-79 and 1988-91). Fiscal adjustment, moreover, was not always accompanied by appreciable decreases in the rate of inflation (Chile in 1974-75, Mexico in 1982-85 and Colombia in 1985-86) (Figures 2.1, 2.2a and b, 2.7, and 2.8).

The weak correspondence or lack of correlation between the rate of inflation and the fiscal deficit is explained by three factors with important implications for the management of public finances.

Because of the dependence of public finances on revenue from major commodities exports, the trend of the fiscal balance in certain countries tends to be anticyclical. When the autonomous fiscal policy is not neutral with respect to such changes, the deterioration of public finances occurs in periods of sluggish economic activity and falling inflation rates; conversely, improvement in the fiscal accounts coincides with the resurgence of demand, which generates economic recovery and speeds up inflation.

This fact points to the need to establish automatic mechanisms to stabilize the level of the real exchange rate and public spending, regardless of changes in the prices of the major commodities exported. In addition, the goals of the

Figure 2.2a. Chile: Inflation and Exchange Rate, 1971-80
(Percentage variation)

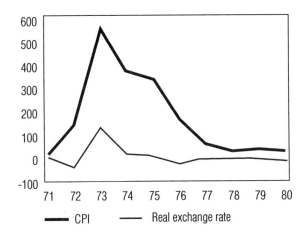

Figure 2.2.b. Chile: Inflation and Exchange Rate, 1981-90
(Percentage variation)

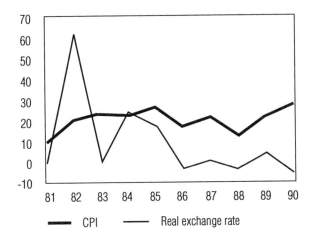

Figure 2.3. Argentina: External and Fiscal Surplus, 1971-90
(Percentages of GDP)

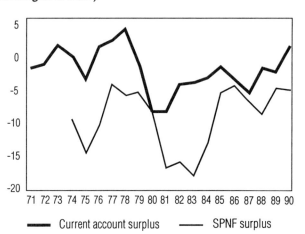

stabilization programs must take these cyclical characteristics into account in order to prevent cyclical trends in public finances. Neither the governments nor multilateral organizations have paid enough attention to this problem, which is analyzed in the following section.

Inflationary inertia, caused by shortening the term of contracts and by the generalized use of indexation clauses and procedures based on the previous period's inflation rates, rendered conventional stabilization programs (based exclusively on fiscal and monetary adjustment) inefficient and determined the effect of changes in the real exchange rate (and of relative prices in general) on the rates of inflation. The degree of indexation in each economy depends on its inflationary history. This and other differences of a structural and cyclical nature, as well as the specific characteristics of exchange management, made the inflationary impact of devaluation different in the various countries (greater in Argentina and Mexico) and, in Chile and Colombia, caused it to vary according to the circumstances.

Consequently, countries with high inflation rates (Argentina, Mexico, and until the early 1980s, Chile) and a high degree of indexation instituted conventional stabilization programs, wherein fiscal and monetary adjustment was accompanied by a fixed exchange rate and the implementation of price and wage policies. In technical publications, elements of this type have been considered an essential complement of the conventional components of a successful and efficient stabilization program, at least in countries that have experienced high inflation rates (see, for example, Kigel [1992] and Bruno, *et al.* [1988]; see also the section entitled "Indexation and Inflationary Inertia," later in this chapter).

Figure 2.4a. Argentina: Inflation and Exchange Rate, 1971-80
(Percentage variation)

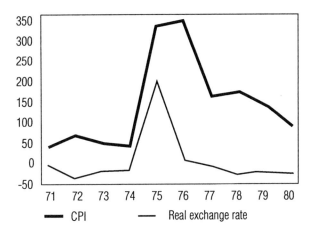

Figure 2.4b. Argentina: Inflation and Exchange Rate, 1981-90
(Percentage variation)

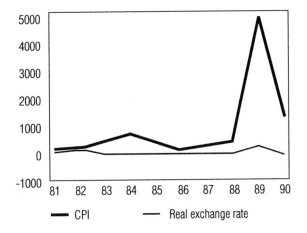

Figure 2.5. Mexico: External and Fiscal Surplus, 1971-90
(Percentages of GDP)

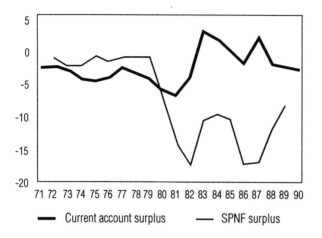

Figure 2.6. Mexico: Inflation and Exchange Rate, 1971-90
(Percentage variation)

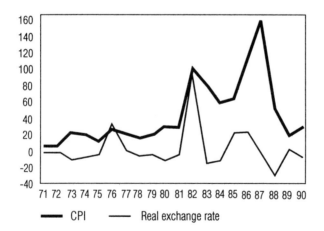

Figure 2.7. Colombia: External and Fiscal Surplus, 1971-90
(Percentages of GDP)

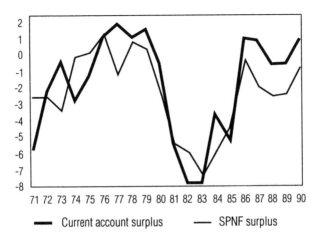

Figure 2.8. Colombia: Inflation and Exchange Rate, 1971-90
(Percentage variation)

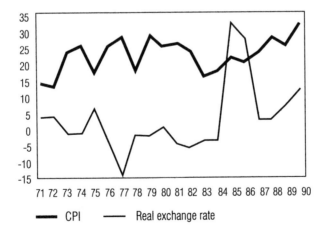

The above was not enough, however, when the countries had accumulated considerable domestic debt, given the persistence of fiscal and quasifiscal deficits (Argentina and Mexico). In these cases, conventional stabilization programs were not successful until measures aimed at reducing the burden of domestic and external debt were adopted. (This subject is discussed later in this chapter in the section entitled "Consequences of a Prolonged Fiscal Deficit: Overindebtedness.")

The implementation of conventional stabilization programs led to complex dilemmas in exchange and fiscal management. In particular, exchange appreciation, due to the slow convergence of domestic and international inflation rates, can eventually cause an exchange crisis, as occurred in Argentina in 1981 and 1988 and in Chile in 1981. Moreover, in the countries that had faced or were in the process of making structural adjustments, exchange appreciation conflicted with the efficient attainment of the objectives of trade liberalization and the control of prices for deregulation and privatization purposes.

Fiscal imbalance in an open economy has more immediate effects on the external balance, both in the current account (since there are no quantitative controls on imports) and especially in the capital account. This problem was aggravated in 1991 by the inflow of capital, which exerted additional pressure on the exchange rate. Countries such as Chile and Colombia, which had chosen stable exchange rate parity, discovered the ineffectiveness of monetary policy in these circumstances and the need for fiscal overadjustment while the net inflow of capital continued. (These subjects are discussed later in this chapter in the section entitled "The Exchange-Fiscal Dilemma in Open Economies.")

Finally, the section entitled "Adjustment, Investment and Growth " analyzes the impact of the crisis and the fiscal adjustment on investment and growth rates during the decade.

Public Finances and External Cycles

In the countries studied, with the exception of Argentina, the factors that generate positive or negative external shocks have similar effects on the fiscal balance. The reason for this is that in these three countries, a substantial proportion of the nonfinancial public sector's current revenues consisted of earnings from their major commodities exports: petroleum and natural gas taxes and the PEMEX operating surplus in Mexico; copper company taxes and operating surpluses in Chile; the operating surpluses of FNC and ECOPETROL (and CARBOCOL and ECONIQUEL), royalties, and taxes on the oil industry and on coffee in Colombia. Thus, the greater value of these exports (resulting from increases in their international prices or in the volume exported), while generating trade surpluses, also tends to generate fiscal surpluses, and the opposite occurs when the value of exports decreases.

Thus, if, in a situation of equilibrium, the external price of oil (coffee or copper) falls temporarily and the reduction in export earnings causes a current account deficit and a fiscal deficit of the same size, macroeconomic equilibrium will remain intact without any change in other variables such as the real exchange rate or public spending. If public spending is reduced in response to a decrease in tax receipts, although in a smaller proportion, a fiscal deficit will occur along with a slowdown in the pace of economic activity and, if a situation of disequilibrium exists, a reduction in the rate of inflation. Exactly the opposite occurs when the price of the good in question rises. This is one of the main reasons for the lack of correlation between the cycles of the fiscal balance and those of the inflationary trend in countries such as Chile and Colombia. In Mexico, where similar conditions exist, the appearance of fiscal deficits caused by this type of external shocks has coincided with enormous devaluations, related to the same cause, and the latter have had an inflationary impact (see the section entitled "Indexation and Inflationary Inertia").

Moreover, owing to the importance of these tax receipts, the public sector becomes a net exporter of goods and services, and, consequently, devaluation of the real exchange rate improves the fiscal balance while at the same time improving the external balance. In short, in these countries is observed an anticyclical, endogenous trend in public finances, which moderates the effects of external shocks on economic activity, along with a positive fiscal effect of real devaluation that facilitates the adjustment processes.

The effectiveness of these endogenous factors depends on the reaction of the autonomous fiscal policy since the government can nullify or reduce their effect if it responds to the generation (or contraction) of temporary, nonrecurrent tax receipts by increasing (or cutting) expenditures.

When there are no pre-established mechanisms for saving surpluses, governments find it difficult to avoid the pressure—or temptation— to spend some or all of the temporary surplus and the increased borrowing capacity it entails. In Mexico in 1980-82, the fiscal deficit actually worsened, despite the enormous increase in petroleum tax receipts. The same thing occurred in Ecuador, Peru, and Venezuela during the oil boom of 1974-81. Even when such mechanisms are present, if the rules governing them are discretionary, it is difficult to save all of the temporary surplus (as was the case in Colombia during the coffee boom of 1976-80).

Similarly, when these nonrecurrent revenues decrease and no resources accumulated during booms are available, or access to external credit is limited (which is generally the case in such periods), the level of public spending cannot be maintained. The situation worsens if rigid rules are imposed with regard to quantitative fiscal deficit objectives, as is true of many programs negotiated with the International Monetary Fund (IMF) without considering these cyclical components or cycles of highs or lows in tax receipts derived from commodities exports.

In these conditions, the trend of public finances magnifies the consequences of external shocks on aggregate demand. In open economies, such as most of those in Latin America today, temporary changes in the prices of their principal export product can have a double destabilizing impact, by generating the two, mutually-reinforcing effects described below:

• A cyclical pattern in the real exchange rate, which creates considerable uncertainty in private sector investments, especially in the tradable goods sector. This pattern can have an effect of the "Dutch disease " type: excessive investment in a commodity due to a temporary upswing in its price and deterioration of the manufacturing industry and other activities that produce tradable goods and services, caused by increases in the relative prices of nontradable goods as a result of appreciation of the local currency in reaction to the increase in external income. This set of circumstances renders the external sector vulnerable to a subsequent fall in the price of the commodity, which can lead to severe exchange crises.
• A cyclical pattern in public spending (and in the behavior of private producers of the commodity, such as coffee growers in Colombia) in response to the level of both economic activity and the price index, with the resultant effects on the external balance and the level of investment. A disparity can also exist between the costs associated with drastic cuts in public spending when the international prices of commodities fall (suspension of programs and investments in progress, layoffs, reductions in real wages, etc.) and the additional spending that occurs during boom periods (marginal or scarcely researched programs and projects, excessive increases in employment or wages, etc.).

The greater instability and uncertainty caused by these changes can have effects on long-term growth rates, chiefly as a result of their impact on investment. Consequently, they can affect the standard of living by reducing the average level of per capita consumption and by causing changes in said variable over time.

The objective must therefore be to establish stabilizing mechanisms that moderate the effect of changes in commodities prices on the real exchange rate and public spending (and the behavior of Colombian coffee growers) and, consequently, on the levels of consumption and investment. Two of the countries studied responded to this challenge, but only partially: Colombia with respect to coffee receipts and Chile with respect to copper receipts.[17]

In Colombia, the government and the coffee growers association set the

---

[17] Venezuela established on Oil Stabilization Fund in the first half of 1992 and had experimented previously with the Venezuelan Investment Fund, which invested abroad some of the surpluses generated during the oil boom in the 1970s.

trigger price (for purchasing some of the crop) on behalf of the FNC. The FNC receives income from the so-called retention quota (a variable percentage of the refund price of coffee exports, which is paid in cash or in kind) and the ad-valorem tax on exports, and can generate profits or losses on direct coffee exports, depending on the relationship between the purchase price and the export price. The government and the association agree on the use of the Fund's surpluses: for sterilization purposes, to finance public investment, for the expenses of the coffee growers committees—on physical or social infrastructure in the coffee growing regions—or for other real or financial investments of the Fund. The uses of these surpluses varied significantly in the different boom periods.

During the 1976–80 boom, much of the increase in the international price was passed on to producers, and although the other aspects of the economic policy were managed anticyclically, the unmistakable effects of Dutch disease could not be avoided. The disease took the form of excessive investment in coffee (which seriously complicated macroeconomic management during the subsequent fall of prices), the crowding out of public and private investment in other sectors (especially the manufacturing industry) and the increased vulnerability of the external sector (as a result of the decline of other activities that produce tradable goods and services) and of public finances (through erosion of the taxes on domestic business activity).

The decision to pass on a substantial portion of the increase in the international price of coffee to producers, given the existence of a new, more productive variety, led to an enormous increase in planting and installed capacity, and the upturn in income caused a rise in the consumption of coffee growers. Anticyclical management of the other aspects of the macroeconomic policy moderated, but could not prevent, some of the effects of Dutch disease.

In fact, to compensate for the increase in aggregate demand and the monetary pressures created by the accumulation of international reserves, public investment was drastically reduced and credit was so tightly restricted as to cause a decrease in private investment in activities other than coffee. The excessive investment in coffee seriously complicated macroeconomic management when the boom ended, since in response to the fall of international prices and the lowering of export quotas under the International Coffee Agreement, the FNC had to continue buying the entire harvest and accumulating enormous stocks, with the result that its position changed from a surplus of 1.85 percent and 1.61 percent of GDP in 1979 and 1980 to a deficit in 1981, creating severe liquidity problems.

In addition, a decision was taken in 1978 to permit gradual appreciation of the exchange rate (the revaluation of the peso between 1976 and 1979 was nearly 25 percentage points) in order to curb the inflationary pressures generated by the accumulation of international reserves. In addition, imports were partially decontrolled, which further weakened the sectors that produce other tradable goods and generated a growing current account deficit once the boom ended. Finally, during the boom period, domestic tax receipts (which decreased as a percentage of GDP, partly as a result of the tax reforms of 1977 and 1979) were replaced by tax receipts from the external sector (taxes on coffee and imports), which then had to be lowered drastically at the end of the boom.

The "miniboom" of 1986 was managed differently. Less of the external price increase was passed on to producers and the growth of surpluses augmented the liquidity of FNC (so that it could easily purchase the harvest during years of changing prices, until the collapse of the International Coffee Agreement drove prices below the record lows). The surpluses were sterilized in the central bank and helped reduce external public debt, without putting pressure on domestic interest rates. Investments in coffee increased very modestly and the process of real devaluation and fiscal adjustment on the revenue side continued. Thus, there was no crowding-out effect on other public or private investments, and the structural weakening of the external sector and of public finances that occurred during the previous boom was avoided.

In recent years, Colombia's public finances have become more dependent on oil receipts (3.3 percent of GDP in 1980) than on coffee receipts, and this trend will certainly intensify as a result of the recent discoveries. In 1991, it was decreed that any ECOPETROL earnings in excess of a certain price could only be used for investments and to pay the debts of other energy sector companies.

In 1981, Chile passed into law a rule governing the spending of copper receipts, according to which income corresponding to prices above a "reference price" could only be used to service public debt (in 1989 it was decided that the Fund's resources could only be used for nonrecurrent public debt payments) or "other purposes specified by law."[18] In 1985, as one of the conditions of the structural adjustment loan (SAL I) granted by the World Bank, the Copper Stabilization Fund (FEC) was established as an account in the central bank, with the purpose of ensuring the stability of the real exchange rate. The agreement with the bank stipulates that if the international price of copper remains within a band close to a "reference price," there will be no deposits to or withdrawals from the Fund;[19] a move into another band will result in a 50 percent marginal deposit (or withdrawal), and beyond that a marginal deposit or withdrawal of 100 percent.

As it happens, the existing Chilean legislation, as well as the design of the FEC and of Colombia's Oil Stabilization Fund, contain a number of flaws:

---

[18] The reference price is defined as the variable, six-year average of the "cash" price on the London metals markets, adjusted for variations in the U.S. consumer price index.

[19] The reference price in this case is an initial fixed price in dollars, adjusted according to an international index of inflation.

• Neither the Chilean law nor the Colombian decree establishes a clear procedure for making withdrawals from the Fund when the international prices of the mineral are low in order to avoid an excessive cut in public spending.[20]

• There is no possibility of the Fund borrowing money to fulfill its purpose when withdrawals are necessary and the amount in the Fund is insufficient.

• The deposit and withdrawal rules do not take into account the level of net assets (or net liabilities) accumulated by the Fund, nor the price of the mineral, which could prevent an erroneous projection of the long-term trend of the price from causing the Fund to accumulate external assets or liabilities indefinitely (or the need to change the rules of the Fund from time to time to prevent this from happening).[21]

• The rules utilize "reference prices" based on historic averages and not on estimates of the price cycle of the mineral. It can be shown that if econometric projections statistically superior to those provided by a random projection are not available, there should be no deposits to or withdrawals from the Fund (Meller, 1992). Nor do they take into account the degree of uncertainty in its future prices.

Once stabilizing mechanisms with clear and appropriate rules are in place, an assessment of the fiscal balance (structural) should be made, excluding the variations in public revenues caused by the price cycles of these commodities and concerning which quantitative fiscal objectives are established in stabilization and macroeconomic management programs.

Indexation and Inflationary Inertia

As indicated above, the correlation between devaluation and inflation has been closer in Argentina and Mexico and less pronounced in Colombia and Chile. In Argentina, the devaluations of 1975, 1982, 1985 and 1989 had a definite inflationary effect. In particular, the exchange adjustment of 1982, which was essential to eliminate the huge current account deficit incurred in the preceding period (above 8 percent of GDP in 1980 and 1981), caused immediate acceleration of the inflationary trend, which led to additional nominal devaluations and a race between prices and exchange rates. In Mexico, the devaluations of 1977, 1982, 1983 and 1986 all accelerated inflation.

---

[20] Moreover, since nearly all of the income of the FEC was spent on the regular service of domestic public debt with the central bank, no resources would have been available to meet a contingency of this nature. In the case of Colombia's FEP, the reference price was set so high that to date it has had no income at all.

[21] *External Shocks and Stabilization Mechanisms*, edited by E. Engel and P. Meller, shows that the most effective rules take these two variables into account.

In Chile, the devaluations of 1974 and 1975 also accelerated the inflationary trend. The same thing happened, although to a lesser extent, with the devaluation of 1983. Nevertheless, throughout the 1983–88 period, a deliberate policy of real depreciation was pursued (for the purpose of fully implementing the structural changes that were to accompany trade liberalization) and this process coincided with a decrease in the rates of inflation from 1986.

In Colombia, real devaluation contributed to acceleration of the inflationary trend between 1970 and 1974. The same thing happened with the acceleration of inflation in the late 1980s. In 1975, however, there was a real devaluation of approximately 7 percent (the aim of which was to compensate for the reduction of export subsidies), while at the same time the rate of inflation fell from 26 to 18 percent per annum. In 1985 and 1986, real devaluations of 32 and 28 percent occurred, respectively, and the rate of inflation moved only slightly, from 18 percent in 1984 to 22 percent in 1985 and to 21 percent in 1986.

The inflationary effect of a devaluation is due, first of all, to the fact that the increase it causes in the prices of tradable goods is transmitted to wages and other prices via propagating mechanisms associated with the processes of creating expectations, the indexation of contracts and negotiating practices. Consequently, the differences in behavior noted above are due in part to the way that these propagating mechanisms work and how the exchange adjustment is carried out.

In an economy such as Argentina's, with a long history of high and varying inflation rates, the propagating mechanisms are more dispersed and operate more immediately since the economic agents have adapted their behavior by shortening the term of wage and price contracts[22] and linking them (and their renegotiation) to the previous period's inflation rate, there being no better basis for their inflation expectations than the last period (Fanelli *et al.*, 1992). In Argentina in the mid-1980s, the adjustment period was no more than a month in most labor, financial and sales contracts. In these conditions, any increase in costs, such as might result from a nominal devaluation, is immediately transmitted in the following month to almost all wages and prices in the economy.

Conversely, when the term of wage and price contracts is a year or more, as in Colombia, inflation expectations are not as closely linked to the previous year's results and, in addition, the effects of an increase in the rate of devalua-

---

[22] Thus, while in an economy such as Colombia's the effective period of the nominal wages agreed to in labor contracts is one or two years, in Argentina it averaged four months in 1981 and one month in 1985, before the implementation of the Austral Plan. Similarly, although in Colombia there are time deposits with a three-month fixed interest rate, in Argentina there was no deposit with a fixed interest rate, not even for a month, before the Austral Plan. Likewise, although most of the industries in Colombia adjust prices no more than once or twice a year, in Argentina in the mid-1980s prices were being adjusted at least once or twice a month.

tion (or any other cost stimulus) are due to the change in relative prices over the entire period. In these circumstances, the shock is spread more slowly—and probably to a lesser degree—to other prices and wages.

The effect of the exchange rate on the propagating mechanisms also depends very much on its direct impact on the prices of wage goods. When the worker's basket of goods consists largely of tradable goods (as in Argentina and Mexico, where most foods are imported or are export products) a nominal devaluation causes an immediate, substantial drop in real wages[23] that immediately sparks a distributive conflict, especially when wages are adjusted in short periods. Devaluation—particularly a massive devaluation—becomes a clear signal of a general increase in prices and, consequently, wipes out all adjustments of prices and real wages. This does not happen when most of the wage goods have no direct impact on the exchange rate, as in Colombia (where many foods and other goods and services in the worker's basket are not traded internationally in any significant quantities); neither workers nor other economic agents view increases in nominal devaluation as an indicator of the expected rate of inflation.

How the exchange adjustment is carried out also helps explain the differences in its inflationary effects. The cases mentioned above, of Argentina and Mexico (and Chile in 1974, 1975 and 1982), involved massive nominal devaluations, which are bound to create expectations. Conversely, successful and efficient real devaluations in Colombia in 1975 and in 1985–86 and in Chile from 1983 on were accomplished by repegging (crawling peg), which is far less likely to create expectations. Moreover, in Colombia, the repegging was not foreseen and the economic agents became aware of it only after a considerable delay.

Finally, the inflationary impact of devaluation will certainly be greater or lesser, all else being equal, depending on the macroeconomic environment in which it takes place, the macroeconomic policy that accompanies it, and the starting point of the inflationary trend. Thus, in Argentina, the devaluations of 1975, 1982 and 1989 coincided with large fiscal deficits and even increased them since the Argentinean public sector is a net importer of goods and services. In Mexico, the devaluations of 1982 and 1986 also occurred when there was a considerable fiscal deficit, which did not contract sufficiently. On both occasions, moreover, the external shocks that made the devaluation necessary also caused substantial erosion of the fiscal accounts.

In Colombia, however, real devaluation was carried out in tandem with a considerable fiscal adjustment and a very strict monetary policy, both in 1975 and in 1985–86. Nevertheless, in the late 1980s, the policy of real devaluation

---

[23] This structural characteristic is also responsible for the greater initial recessive effect of devaluation, in comparison with a case such as Colombia's.

accelerated the rate of inflation, despite fiscal equilibrium and the implementation of a strict monetary policy. To explain these very different results, it has been suggested that although devaluation in the earlier period led to macroeconomic equilibrium because there was a substantial exchange lag, at the end of the decade the exchange rate was raised artificially—as a deliberate step to prepare for the opening up of the economy—to a level that was not compatible with macroeconomic equilibrium, or that would have been only if there were a large fiscal surplus (World Bank, 1992a). It is not easy, however, to determine the equilibrium exchange rate in an economy that has just embarked on an ambitious trade liberalization and tax abatement process and which is receiving a considerable but possibly temporary inflow of capital.

In Chile, the evidence is even less clear in this regard. In 1974–75, devaluation was accompanied by an impressive fiscal adjustment, but it still did not prevent runaway inflation. In contrast, the policy of real appreciation pursued from 1983 on coincided, in its early years, with the largest fiscal deficits of the period and with a lax monetary policy aimed at keeping interest rates down, and yet, the sum of these factors did not significantly affect the rates of inflation.

The following are possible reasons for this extraordinary phenomenon:

• The rate of inflation had already been reduced to less than 10 percent in 1981, and from 1982 the wage indexation mechanisms were abolished and collective bargaining was suspended.
• The level of utilization of the installed capacity was very low to start with (so that the expansion of aggregate demand produced an immediate reaction in the level of economic activity).
• The fiscal and quasifiscal deficits were not financed with a currency issue, but rather with debt instruments that were placed directly, without putting additional pressure on interest rates.
• The initial level of public debt was very low and when it had grown significantly, a fiscal adjustment was made and quasifiscal operations were terminated, so that no symptoms of overindebtedness appeared as they had in Argentina and Mexico (see the later section entitled "Consequences of a Prolonged Fiscal Deficit: Overindebtedness").
• Finally, deterioration of the fiscal balance was offset by a spectacular increase in private saving, thanks to the strong presence of exports and, possibly, to the effects of the social insurance reform of 1980 and the tax reform of 1984, so that the external balance did not deteriorate and the level of private investment was unaffected.

As a result of the existing degree of indexation, all of the countries that had experienced high inflation in the last two decades found it necessary to utilize exchange anchors and wage and price policies as part of their anti-inflationary strategy. This was true in Chile in 1976–81, in Mexico from 1988 on, and in Argentina in 1976–81 and in 1985, following implementation of the Austral Plan, the Primavera Plan, the Erman Plans, and the Cavallo Plan.

The results of these programs were also uneven. Domestic and international rates of inflation converged more slowly when the stabilization program was not accompanied by an appropriate wage and price policy (as in Chile from 1976 to 1981, where wages were linked to the rate of domestic inflation), when it was carried out in conditions of fiscal disequilibrium (as in Argentina from 1976 to 1981 and from 1987 to 1990), or when the size and weight of public debt created expectations of a devaluation or of an implicit or explicit repudiation of public debt (Mexico until 1989 and Argentina until 1990).

The Exchange-Fiscal Dilemma in Open Economies

The slow convergence of domestic and international rates of inflation creates a dilemma since the resulting appreciation can lead to an exchange crisis, as was the case in Argentina in 1981 and 1988 and in Chile in 1981. In the current conditions, this danger seems remote because of the considerable inflow of capital. In the medium term, the stability of the process will depend on how fast inflation rates converge, whether the capital flows are temporary or permanent and whether they finance increases in investment or increases in consumption. At any rate, the current inflow is the result of a reshuffling of the portfolios of the economic agents, prompted both by factors of expulsion (the recession and falling interest rates in the United States) and of attraction (through improvement in the prospects of the Latin American economies), but as soon as it exceeds the increased demand for money that reshuffling implies, inflationary pressures and further exchange rate appreciation can result (Cline, 1992).

The success of structural reform processes aimed at reorientation of the productive sectors toward tradable goods and the country's comparative advantages can be compromised by exchange appreciation. This is a problem for both Chile and Colombia, where the inflow of capital has exerted pressure on the exchange rate. In these circumstances, these two countries chose to protect the stability of exchange parity. They also tried, at least initially, to alleviate the inflationary pressures caused by the accumulation of international reserves with a strict monetary policy. The resultant jump in interest rates, however, became an additional stimulus to the inflow of capital, so that the pressure on the exchange rate continued, monetary control became less effective, the central banks incurred substantial debt, the quasifiscal deficit increased and the subsequent implementation of monetary policy was made more difficult. In Chile the debt accumulated by the central bank substantially limited its scope of action, and in Colombia a process of "endogenization" of the money supply occurred, which was very similar to what happened in Argentina and Mexico with respect to overindebtedness.

This experience led both countries to concentrate their anti-inflationary efforts on fiscal policy, so that while the inflow of short-term capital continues, a fiscal surplus large enough to protect exchange parity is maintained. The two countries also relaxed their exchange controls to permit modest appreciation— not so much as to jeopardize the objectives of structural reform, but enough to boost the credibility of the exchange policy and to help curb inflationary pressures without resorting to an excessive fiscal overadjustment, which could cause a recession.

Argentina and Mexico, on the other hand, have preferred anti-inflationary objectives, even though they cause appreciation of the local currency. In Mexico, this decision was based on the conviction that the inflow of capital is permanent, at least in part, since it was stimulated by economic integration with the U.S. markets. The argument, in these circumstances, is that Mexico will attract a significant flow of foreign investments for many years, as Spain and Portugal did when they joined the European Community. The decision was also based on the expectation that this integration will result in a more rapid convergence of domestic and international inflation rates. In any case, in the second stage of the stabilization plan, Mexico switched from a fixed exchange rate to a moving peg, with a rate below the difference between the domestic and international rates of inflation in order to reduce the degree of appreciation of the peso and lend greater credibility to its exchange policy.

In Argentina, there is less reason to think that the current inflow of capital is permanent and, therefore, the process of appreciation involves greater risks if domestic and international rates of inflation do not converge. Recent analysis indicates that residual inflation in the 20 percent range persists as a result of certain inertial factors and despite the attainment of a higher level of de-indexation than in earlier programs (Fanelli, *et al.*, 1992). In these circumstances, the current practice of fixing the exchange rate by law could seriously complicate the transfer to a moving peg system, as occurred in Mexico.

The convertibility law and the practice of legally fixing the exchange rate render the economy extremely vulnerable to external shocks. In these circumstances, the necessary depreciation of the real exchange rate will require a nominal decrease in domestic wages and prices, which hardly seems likely in a modern economy and even less so in one with an inflationary history such as Argentina's. In these conditions, the extent of the recession necessary for the external adjustment would entail enormous economic and social costs and would cause an acute crisis in the financial sector. As it happens, the gold standard and other currency board experiments failed in the past precisely because of the nonviability of deflationary adjustments to external shocks.

It must be admitted, however, that Argentina's situation, after two episodes of hyperinflation, required that expectations be subjected to a shock of the kind produced by the increased stringency of the exchange and monetary policy.

The convertibility law undoubtedly reinforced the credibility of the policy, at least initially. It must also be remembered that devaluation in Argentina has a negative fiscal effect, so that there are two reasons for using the exchange rate as an anti-inflationary tool, unlike the other cases studied.

Consequences of a Prolonged Fiscal Deficit: Overindebtedness

Nonviability of a Persistent Fiscal Deficit Financed with Debt

The experiences of Mexico and Argentina show that a prolonged fiscal deficit causes instability, even after it has been eliminated, and that successful and efficient stabilization programs must therefore include a substantial reduction of the burden (stock and flow) of public debt.

In 1981, Sargent and Wallace (1985) demonstrated that a persistent fiscal deficit leads to an explosive accumulation of public debt and that, in such circumstances, monetary policy becomes ineffective as a means of controlling inflation. According to their argument, if the real interest rate exceeds the rate of economic growth, the following dilemma arises: to be able to refinance government debt, resources must be found to pay the interest, so that the government has to increase the primary surplus, issue currency or contract new debt. Incurring new debt, however, signifies a real increase in government debt as a percentage of GDP, which cannot continue indefinitely.[24] Sooner or later the government will be forced either to issue currency to service the debt or not pay it. Consequently, without an adequate fiscal adjustment or debt relief, the use of monetary policy to fight inflation inevitably leads to higher inflation rates in the future or debt repudiation.[25]

Expectations of Overindebtedness, Devaluation and the Rates of Inflation and Interest: The Mexican Experience

Before arriving at this situation, however, the public demands higher or more indexed real interest rates to guard against these risks, which discourages investment, puts inflationary pressure on costs and accelerates the explosive growth of domestic debt, thus jeopardizing the short-term achievements of the stabilization programs. The Mexican experience is a case in point.

The initially high level of domestic public debt in Mexico and the need to increase it to finance the net flow of financial transfers abroad, determined by

---

[24] In an open economy, moreover, high real interest rates attract capital flows that complicate the monetary problem and exert upward pressure on the exchange rate.

[25] This argument was advanced in 1981 in the classic article by Sargent and Wallace.

agreements with the international financial system following the suspension of external payments in October 1982, created in the private sector expectation that the government might have to resort to inflationary financing, higher taxes or the repudiation of external or domestic debt. In these circumstances, the inflation and devaluation expectations persisted, domestic interest rates climbed and capital flight continued. These facts contributed to the persistence of the inflationary trend and the low levels of private investment (which, together with the reduction in public investment, impeded the recovery of growth), despite the impressive fiscal and external adjustments carried out during those years. In particular, higher rates on public debt created an even greater need for domestic financing to cover the overall fiscal deficit and, consequently, required a larger primary fiscal overadjustment.

In fact, the stabilization programs introduced in response to the external shocks sustained by the Mexican economy in the 1980s were based on a sizable fiscal adjustment, which permitted a transition from primary deficits of approximately 7.3 percent of GDP in 1982 to a surplus of 4.23 percent in 1983 and more than 7.5 percent in 1988 and 1989. Nevertheless, it was not until 1989 that inflation could be significantly lowered and a modest recovery of economic growth initiated.

The fiscal and exchange adjustments of 1983 were very effective in bringing about the external adjustment: from current account deficits of 6.4 percent in 1981 and 3.6 percent in 1982, there was a 3.6 percent surplus in 1983. In fact, given the relative stability of the private sector balance throughout the period, the changes in the current account appear to be closely related to the public sector balance. This result is due in part to the fact that real devaluation, as mentioned above, contributes both to the external adjustment and to the fiscal adjustment.

Nevertheless, the fiscal adjustment did not produce domestic stability. The inflation rate did not fall (from the 59 percent registered in 1982 it rose to 102 percent in 1983 and dropped back to 58 percent in 1985), GDP decreased 5.3 percent in 1983 and the recovery of growth was extremely slight in 1984 and 1985.

The available analyses suggest that the fiscal adjustment was inefficient for three fundamental reasons:

• The inertial components of the inflationary trend had in any case created a situation wherein the contraction of aggregate demand caused by the fiscal and monetary adjustment had a modest effect on the rate of inflation in the short term and, therefore, had a recessive impact.

• Added to this were the inflationary—initially recessive—effects of the nominal devaluation (130 percent in 1982 and 113 percent in 1983).

• The effect of overindebtedness on inflation, devaluation and interest rate expectations.

Between 1982 and 1987, domestic debt grew considerably. Moreover, as a result of the shorter terms and higher domestic interest rates, in 1987 interest payments on domestic public debt absorbed three-fourths of the total tax receipts and were nearly four times larger than the interest payments on external public debt, despite the fact that the latter was still more than twice as large as domestic public debt.

The effect of overindebtedness on the expectations of the economic agents was intensified in 1986 when the oil crisis revealed the fragility of the fiscal and external adjustments achieved in prior years. In reaction to the collapse of the New York stock market in October 1987, the economic agents quickly reorganized their portfolios and the Mexican government was forced to effect another devaluation and to alter its stabilization program.

The transfer of resources abroad as a result of the external debt burden (equivalent to 4.8 percent of GDP on average between 1983 and 1987, despite the debt rescheduling agreements of 1982–83, 1984–85 and 1986–87) caused a substantial decline in total investment with its negative effect on growth rates (see the section later in this chapter entitled "Adjustment, Investment and Growth").

In short, both from the viewpoint of the efficient attainment of stabilization objectives and the perspectives of medium- and long-term growth, it became necessary, in addition to the primary fiscal adjustment, to reduce the size of the external transfer and the fiscal impact of the amount of domestic public debt outstanding.

From 1987 on, unlike the prior period, Mexico enjoyed considerable success both in reducing the rate of inflation (to less than 20 percent a year) and reviving economic growth, thanks to a fortuitous combination of conventional and unconventional economic policy measures. The program introduced in late 1987, taking into account the previous experience, was supposed to be based, in addition to another fiscal adjustment—which brought the primary surplus to 8 percent of GDP—on an income and wage policy (including a fixed exchange rate) designed to break inflationary inertia and thus effect a more efficient adjustment, i.e., a quicker reduction of the inflation rate with less of a sacrifice in terms of growth.

Despite the success in curbing inflation, real domestic interest rates rose in the first two years of the Mexican Pact for Stability and Economic Growth (28.4 percent in 1988 and 29.9 percent in 1989). These high interest rates threatened the success of stabilization by inhibiting investment and, therefore, economic recovery, since they entailed a very high and growing level of domestic debt service. The high interest rates were again due to the lack of credibility of the fixed exchange rate policy and the stabilization program as a whole, because of the enormous weight of external and internal transfers.

In fact, both the differential between the interest rate of the public debt expressed in pesos and the sum of the interest rate of the public debt expressed in dollars and the preannounced devaluation rate, which measures devaluation expectations, and the differential between the interest rate of the debt expressed in dollars and the international interest rate, which measures the risk of explicit repudiation of external debt, increased at the start of the Pact (Oks and Dunn, 1991). Both differentials then decreased substantially, first toward the middle of 1988, when the maturities of domestic debt were first extended,[26] and then around the middle of 1989, when the agreement concluded within the framework of the Brady Plan was announced, which considerably reduced the principal and service of the debt (net financial transfers from Mexico decreased nearly 2 percent of GDP in the 1989–94 period).

The government's ability to service a given stock of debt can be evaluated by comparing the present value of future debt service obligations with that of the primary fiscal surpluses. While the fiscal policy affects the latter, debt management (both domestic and external) determines the former. Available estimates suggest that, in fact, both the larger primary fiscal surplus and the reduction of the debt burden explain the decrease in the differentials between the domestic and external interest rates and those expressed in pesos and dollars.[27]

Both the agreement on external debt and the increase in the maturity profile of domestic debt considerably reduced the short-term payment obligations on Mexican public debt, and the increase in the primary fiscal surplus gave a signal that the government was more able to meet them, so that the two facts together convinced the economic agents that the risk of explicit or implicit repudiation of public debt had been considerably reduced. This change in expectations brought about a sizable reduction in the domestic interest rate (and in the differentials between the domestic and external interest rates), which substantially improved the overall fiscal balance, facilitated increased investment and boosted the credibility of the quasi-fiscal exchange rate policy and the stabilization program as a whole.

Overindebtedness, Exchange Runs, Demonetization and Hyperinflation: The Argentinean Experience

Although the process of fiscal disequilibrium and indebtedness was ongoing, at some point confidence was so low as to cause a run on the local currency in

---

[26] The maturity profile of domestic debt was expanded by introducing Bondes (two- and three-year bonds with floating interest rates linked to 28-day Cetes) in mid-1988, Ajustabonos (bonds linked to 5-year inflation) in late 1989, and redeeming the 28-day Cetes and replacing them with 90-, 180-, and 365-day Cetes in 1990. The changes in the average maturities of the bonds are illustrated in Figure 11 of Oks (1992).

[27] An econometric verification of this hypothesis can be found in Oks, 1992. In addition, the total international reserves should be sufficient to cover a run on the peso (for example, covering the money stock and the short-term domestic debt callable in the short term).

favor of real assets and dollars, which reduced the base of the same inflation tax and necessitated a higher inflation rate to finance the public deficit, even though it was not as large as it had been. In fact, the lower the rate of monetization of the economy the greater the inflationary impact of a given fiscal deficit (not financed externally), since the inflation rate has to be higher for the government to be able to collect the same inflation tax to finance its deficit. For this reason, Argentina experienced a hyperinflationary trend in 1989 but not in 1983, despite the fact that the fiscal deficit was larger in 1983 and the inflation tax was similar in both years (Fanelli *et al.*, 1992). In Argentina, economic and political uncertainty in 1989 caused a contraction of the demand for domestic assets, which, given the persistence of a fiscal and quasi-fiscal deficit of approximately 10 percent of GDP—with domestic financing requirements of around 5 percent of GDP—initiated the hyperinflationary trend.

Monetary policy is ineffective in these circumstances. Increases in the real interest rate undermine confidence instead of bolstering it because they involve larger fiscal deficits and larger debt, which is correctly perceived as nonviable. Moreover, the acceleration of inflation and demonetization adversely affect public finances, neutralizing the effects of the autonomous fiscal policy. This was the case in Argentina during the 1980s, and there were several reasons for it:

- The Oliveira-Tanzi effect on tax receipts.
- The erosion of the tax base.
- The increased difficulty of control.
- The lag of the rates and prices of public enterprises (especially when they were used as anchors in the stabilization plans).
- In addition, the quasifiscal deficit grew in response to the rise in nominal interest rates, due both to the acceleration of the inflationary trend and to increases in the real rates (because of devaluation expectations or the application of a strict monetary policy). In fact, the central bank recognized a variable interest rate on its debt (accumulated to finance the quasifiscal operations it had to carry out at the beginning of the decade to overcome the financial and exchange crisis, and later to support the increasingly difficult domestic financing of the public deficit), and in exchange received fixed rates for most of its credits. This arrangement later became a significant destabilizing factor and contributed decisively to the collapse of the stabilization programs launched in 1984, 1985, 1988, and 1989.

The effects of overindebtedness were intensified by demonetization.[28] In Argentina, as the debt grew and the money stock decreased as a percentage of GDP, all control over the money supply was lost: the public and the banks ob-

---

[28] Demonetization, in turn, is caused by the acceleration of inflationary trends, exchange instability, a persistent fiscal deficit and overindebtedness itself. In fact, to protect against the possible loss

tained the liquidity they wanted by selling some of the domestic debt instruments they held. Given the changes in expectations, these monetary "avalanches" financed acceleration of the inflationary trend or runs on the peso, while the monetary authority stood helplessly by (Barkai, 1992; Beckerman, 1992).

The subsequent failure of the Austral Plan, despite its initial success, was due, among other things, to the reversal of the fiscal adjustment, which was based on temporary increases in public revenues, and to the fact that the problem of overindebtedness was not addressed. Subsequent stabilization plans achieved neither fiscal adjustment nor the reduction of overindebtedness. In contrast, the success of the Cavallo Plan was due, among other things, to the fact that it resulted in a larger and more lasting fiscal adjustment and that it was implemented after the compulsory conversion of domestic debt into BONEXes in early 1990 had restored the effectiveness of the monetary policy (Barkai, 1992). Later, the agreement reached within the framework of the Brady Plan permitted a substantial reduction of the stock of external debt, although it did not reduce the actual flow of payments since Argentina was not fulfilling its obligations in this respect.

The failure of the Austral Plan is attributed to several specific reasons:

• It was not possible to change the short term of contracts or the short-term indexation mechanisms, so that when the controls were lifted, the adjustment of relative prices caused an acceleration of the rate of inflation. The inflationary effect of adjusting relative prices was especially acute in a situation where aggregate demand was subject to upward pressures and where the effect that reducing the rate of inflation would have in terms of triggering demand was underestimated. In these conditions, greater fiscal and monetary austerity were required.

• The fiscal adjustment was incomplete and was based partly on taxes that later had to be eliminated (the increase in export duties), were temporary (forced saving mechanisms), or had temporary effects (increases in energy taxes and prices and other public prices, which, in real terms, subsequently deteriorated).

• In particular, although the deficit of the nonfinancial public sector was substantially reduced and was not financed with a direct currency issue, the same was not true of the quasi-fiscal deficit, which grew both as a consequence of the increased domestic debt needed to finance the nonfinancial public sector

---

of the real value of their wealth, to earn speculative profits on the local currency or to evade the possible inflation tax (or debt repudiation) foreshadowed by the persistent fiscal deficit and overindebtedness, economic agents in Argentina were converting growing portions of their liquid assets into foreign currency. The process of demonetization thus became a structural problem to the extent that with the same inflation rates as in the past (after the Austral Plan), the coefficient of monetization was smaller.

deficit and the generation of extremely high ex-post real interest rates brought about by the slowing of inflation. The increase in the quasi-fiscal deficit became one of the main reasons for currency issues during the period.

• As a result of the domestic financing of the fiscal and quasi-fiscal deficit, overindebtedness kept increasing and, therefore, the problems associated with the "endogenization" of the money supply were exacerbated.

• Some serious problems arose in the external sector. The deterioration of the terms of trade in 1985–86 was nearly 22 percent and the exportable supply of agricultural products shrank. These facts, together with another exchange run, made it necessary to declare a moratorium on external payments in April 1988, which delivered a fatal blow to the credibility of the stabilization program.

In contrast, the Cavallo Plan was more successful than the Austral Plan and earlier plans for several reasons.

• It legally subjected government policy to substantial constraints, which had a very positive effect on private sector expectations (although this is the Achilles' heel of the plan, as indicated in the section entitled "Indexation and Inflationary Inertia").

• It attempted to "de-index" the process of price setting in the economy with greater success than any previous effort by legally prohibiting indexation clauses and the use of the incumbent party's influence against unions.

• The fiscal adjustment is deeper and more permanent than in previous efforts since it is based on the reinforcement of major taxes—VAT and income tax— and the tax administration (and not on minor or temporary taxes), as well as on government reforms aimed at eliminating the structural factors that encourage excessive spending (instead of simple spending cuts).

• It was carried out after a substantial reduction of overindebtedness, thanks to the compulsory conversion of domestic debt into BONEXes in 1990.

The fact that the new stabilization program was the creation of an economic team different from the one that had effected the compulsory conversion of debt prevented the distrust generated by episodes of this type from seriously undermining the credibility of the new program. Moreover, the Brady Plan and privatization permitted a significant reduction in outstanding external debt, but not in the actual interest payments.

• Capital inflows from the sale of public assets also helped temporarily reduce the fiscal deficit by decreasing the need to issue new domestic debt while building a larger, more lasting primary surplus.

• Trade liberalization added the disciplinary effect of greater competition to the process of adjusting the prices of tradable goods and services.

• The greater credibility of the program, the lowering of interest rates and the recession in the United States facilitated a process of capital repatriation that made it possible to finance the growing current account deficit.

Adjustment, Investment and Growth

The rate of investment fell during the last decade in three of the four countries studied: in Argentina from 22 percent of GDP in 1980 to about 12 percent in 1985 and after; in Mexico from 27 percent in 1980 to 20 percent in 1983–84 and 17 percent in 1987; and in Chile from 21 percent to 10 percent in 1983 (followed by a rebound in 1990 to 20 percent of GDP). The exception was Colombia, where gross investment remained between 18 and 20 percent of GDP throughout the decade and—not counting the accumulation of inventories (very high at the start of the decade due to the rise in coffee inventories)—investment in fixed capital increased slightly (Table 2.2).

The most significant reductions in investment rates reflect both the fiscal adjustment effort (public investment fell from 6.4 to 3.3 percent of GDP in Argentina, from 8.8 to 4.8 percent in Mexico and from 5.4 to 4.3 percent in Chile between the beginning and the end of the decade) and the effect of the economic crisis and the adjustment programs themselves on private investment. The latter declined in Argentina, from 16.2 percent of GDP in 1979 to 9.4 percent in 1990; in Mexico it decreased from 18.4 percent in 1980 to 12 percent in 1987; and in Chile public investment slid from 15.6 percent in 1980 to 5.1 percent in 1983 and then climbed to 16 percent in 1992. In Colombia, private investment in fixed capital dropped from 10 percent in 1979 to 8 percent in 1985, while public investment rose from 6 percent to 9 percent and then climbed to 10 percent at the end of the period, while public investment decreased to 8 percent of GDP.

These decreases in private investment during the decade were the result of recessive periods and the increased uncertainty associated with macroeconomic instability (changes in inflation rates, real interest rates and the real exchange rate), which prompted both a disinclination to take risk and a decrease in private saving, while at the same time the fiscal crisis eroded the public surplus and the debt crisis reduced the possibility of transfers of external savings. No wonder, then, that the largest and most lasting decreases in the rates of saving and private investment occurred in Argentina and that the smallest and purely temporary decreases were in Colombia.

Moreover, the rate of gross investment in Colombia did not decrease in the first half of the decade because the drop in the rate of domestic saving prior to 1983–85 was offset by an increase in external saving, facilitated by the accumulation of international reserves in the period before the boom in the external sector and by continued access to external credit. Thus, unlike other Latin American countries, it was only starting in 1986 that the country had to generate a current account surplus and, therefore, only until then did domestic saving have to exceed gross investment. It was able to do this easily and without a decline in the rate of investment, thanks to the increases in public saving (2.6 percent of GDP in 1986) and private saving (which went from 13 percent in 1985 to 14 percent of GDP in 1986 and to over 15 percent in 1988) associated with the coffee boom of 1986, new oil and mining exports, the positive effects of real devaluation on the external and fiscal accounts, and the autonomous fiscal policy measures.

In fact, the modest decline in private investment in the first half of the decade was the result both of the slower pace of economic activity as well as the crowding-out effect caused by growing public investment in conditions of constant aggregate saving. This increased public investment, which was concentrated in energy projects, naturally decreased when the latter ended, and the surpluses derived from increased oil exports contributed decisively to the subsequent recovery of domestic saving. These factors, together with economic revitalization, facilitated the recovery of private investment.

Private investment was also crowded out in other countries, despite the cutback in public investment, as a result of the sharp decrease in aggregate saving during part of the decade. This happened in Argentina, where, due to the severity of the crisis, domestic saving fell from 20 percent of GDP in 1980 to 8 percent, and to 10 percent in 1984 and it became necessary to declare a moratorium on the payment of external interest to force some positive transfer of external savings. Furthermore, given the reduction in credit sources caused by demonetization and inflationary acceleration, the government's excessive demand for loanable funds—even though it abated—had a crowding-out effect on the financing of private investment.

The recovery of private saving and investment in Chile in the presence of large fiscal and quasi-fiscal deficits until 1985—following their spectacular plunge in the crisis early in the decade—warrants further comment. The figures in Table 2.2 indicate that the more than 10 percent decrease in the nonfinancial public sector balance between 1980 and 1984 was more than offset by an increase of 13 percent of GDP in the private balance and permitted an improvement of 3 percent of GDP in the current account. Taking the decade as a whole, the fact that the adjustment of the private balance was achieved more with an increase in saving than through a reduction in investment helps to explain the recovery of economic growth after 1984.

The extraordinary recovery of private saving was related to the fact that much of the growth of the nonfinancial public sector deficit was caused by the social insurance reform and the tax reform of 1984, the aim of which was to encourage private saving. The social insurance reform spurred both private saving and aggregate saving because it involved a switch from a simple pay-as-you-go system to a capitalization system. In fact, some of its resources were obligatorily invested in public bonds, which provided some of the fi-

Table 2.2 Sectoral Balances
(Percentage of GDP)

	Chile				Colombia				Mexico			Argentina			
	1976	1980	1990	1980-90 Minimum	1970	1980	1990	1980-90 Minimum	1980	1987	1980-87 Minimum	1971	1979	1980	1980-90 Minimum
Total investment	12.8	21.0	20.2	9.8 (83)	20.2	19.1	19.5	18.0 (86)	27.2	16.8	16.8 (87)	20.1	22.6	12.7	10.6 (88)
Public FBKF	5.8	5.4	4.3	4.7 (83)	5.6	7.4	8.2	8.1 (83)	8.8	4.8	4.8 (87)	5.7	6.4	3.3	3.3 (89)
Private FBKF	7.0	15.6	15.9	5.1 (83)	12.4	9.4	10.0	8.3 (84)	18.4	12.0	12.0 (87)	14.4	16.2	9.4	5.0 (88)
Change in inventories	—	—	—	—	2.2	2.3	1.3	—	—	—	—	—	—	—	—
National saving	17.1	16.8	23.1	7.1 (82)	16.3	19.6	20.8	14.7 (83)	23.2	19.8	19.2 (82)	18.5	21.8	14.4	8.4 (86)
Public saving¹	9.4	11.0	7.0	1.2 (82)	4.4	4.6	5.7	1.3 (83)	6.1	5.8	1.8 (81)	1.5	-0.2	-1.7	-10.5 (86)
Private saving	7.7	5.8	16.1	5.8 (80)	11.9	15.0	15.1	12.4 (84)	17.1	14.0	14.0 (87)	17.0	21.8	16.1	9.7 (86)
External saving	-4.3	4.2	-2.9	-7.2 (88)	4.0	-0.5	-1.3	-4.0 (86)	4.0	-3.1	-56.0 (81)	1.6	1.0	-1.7	-8.2 (80)

¹ Includes net capital flows in Chile.
Source: Case studies.

nancing for the fiscal deficit generated by the reform itself.[29] No evaluation of the effects of the tax reform of 1984 on saving is available. Nevertheless, since part of the increase observed in private saving was used to amortize debt, it may have been prompted by the tax incentive provided by that reform. Moreover, many of the quasi-fiscal operations were made conditional upon the retirement of liabilities—in other words, increased private saving.

The recovery of economic growth, facilitated by large surpluses of installed capacity and manpower,[30] sparked the resurgence of private investment in 1987, which was easily financed thanks to increases in domestic saving and the end of the fiscal crisis.

The trend of economic growth rates in the four countries in the last decade is related to the differential effects of the crisis and the adjustment programs on the rates of investment. It is also explained by their differential effects on the pattern of effective aggregate demand.

Moreover, since real devaluation has stronger inflationary effects in Argentina and less intense effects in Colombia, its impact on economic activity is directly opposite. This is due both to the greater impact of devaluation on real wages in Argentina, as explained above, and to the weaker response of its exports, given the greater predominance of raw materials and industrial exports (petrochemicals, iron and steel) than in countries such as Chile and Colombia.

The characteristics of the fiscal adjustment also had an effect in this regard. The fact that the adjustment in Colombia was based not on public spending cuts but on an increase in revenue generated by larger oil surpluses and temporary increases in import taxes contributed to its comparatively smaller impact on effective demand. The case in Chile was similar.

---

[29] This, however, led to the accumulation of substantial domestic public debt during the period.
[30] Which help explain why the expensive policy from 1982 on did not generate inflationary pressures.

CHAPTER THREE

FISCAL EFFECTS OF
TRADE LIBERALIZATION

Theory and Trends

Effects on Customs Receipts

The impact of trade liberalization on customs receipts depends on (i) the existing protective structure; (ii) the characteristics and the sequence of the liberalization process; (iii) whether the process is accompanied by an exchange adjustment; and (iv) the response of imports, which is determined in part—but only in part—by the preceding conditions.

Three characteristics of the existing protective structure have a particular impact on the response of imports and customs receipts: (i) the relative weight of the tariffs and the non-tariff restrictions; (ii) the extent of the exemptions; and (iii) the degree of dispersion in the tariff structure.

At one extreme, when the protective system is based on more or less uniform tariffs with few exemptions, the liberalization process will essentially consist of lowering the common tariff, which will almost certainly reduce customs receipts. To prevent this, an extremely rigorous exchange adjustment must be effected simultaneously, prompted by considerations other than trade liberalization (such as the existence of a substantial exchange deficit prior to liberalization).[31]

Conversely, when the protective system consists primarily of non-tariff restrictions which are lifted at the start of the liberalization process, provided that the tax abatement process is gradual, customs receipts may increase in the short term since the fiscal effect of the increase in imports may exceed that of the initial lowering of tariffs.

If, in addition, there is considerable dispersion in the tariff structure, higher tariffs may be applied to those imports that respond most favorably to liberalization (imports of final consumption goods) and, consequently, the change in the composition of imports will boost the average real tariff (ratio of real receipts to the value of imports), although the average nominal tariff will decrease. This will also occur if, in the initial stage, tariff exemptions are eliminated. Moreover, tariff restrictions can initially be replaced by tariffs, which will push the average real tariff even higher.

Customs receipts and other taxes on imports represented 1.1 percent (Argentina), 1.2 percent (Mexico) and 1.6 percent (Colombia and Chile) of GDP in the early 1970s. This low level was due both to the relative degree of closure of the economies, measured by the import/GDP ratio, and the predominance of non-tariff measures in the protective policies as well as the extent of the exemptions (imports by the public sector and by certain industrial sectors and other activities accorded preferential treatment). The latter created considerable disparity between the average real tariff and the average nominal tariff.

Generally, both the indices of openness and the average real tariffs were lower in the larger countries of the region (Argentina, Brazil and Mexico), as a result both of their larger economies and the rigor and characteristics of their protective policies. In smaller, more open countries, where tariffs were favored as a means of protection for fiscal reasons (since there was less capacity to collect taxes on domestic activity), the ratios between customs receipts and GDP were higher (3.3 percent in Guatemala and 3.4 percent in Costa Rica in the early 1980s) (ECLAC, 1990). Countries such as Chile and Colombia ranked in the middle.

These facts, and the weight of the larger countries, explain why Latin America, on average, has a customs receipts/GDP ratio well below the corresponding average for other Third World areas (where the protective system consists

---

[31] In fact, receipts would decrease if the percentage increase in the value of imports in local currency were not greater than the percentage decrease in the average tariff, which would require either a very substantial, simultaneous exchange adjustment or an improbably high level of short-term price elasticity. Thus, if the average real tariff were cut in half, the value of imports in local currency would have to be doubled, which would require more than doubling the real exchange rate (since the imports/GDP ratio would decrease, given a comparable exchange adjustment) or, if exchange parity were maintained, a short-term price-elasticity equal to (1 + Ao)/(A1-Ao) (for example, equal to 6 if the tariff falls from 40 to 20 percent).

chiefly of tariffs and there are fewer exemptions), as every international comparison of tax structures has revealed (Tanzi, in Bird and Oldman, 1990).

Consequently, the potential importance of the loss of customs receipts as a result of trade liberalization was less for the large and even the medium-sized countries of Latin America, in contrast to the experience of countries in other regions[32] and the smaller countries of the region itself. These characteristics of their protective systems were such that customs receipts increased with liberalization, or decreased very little, at least initially, insofar as the impact of liberalization (lifting of non-tariff restrictions) and the elimination of exemptions on the response and composition of imports and, finally, on the trend of receipts, was greater and more immediate than the impact of tax abatement. This is precisely what happened in several of the cases studied.

Other factors can also affect the trend of average real tariffs. Reducing the amount of contraband can slow their decline. Subregional integration processes, which have accelerated with the new economic policy orientation in Latin America, cause further deterioration.

The response of imports depends, in addition to the above, on other factors. Thus, for example, the existence of an oligopolistic market initially prevents the reduction of tariffs from being passed on to consumers and suppresses the response of imports. The same thing occurs when an economy is tightly closed and there are no distribution channels other than those open to national producers. It takes time for other economic agents to develop a distribution system that will permit a substantial increase in competitive imports.

Exchange management also affects the outcome considerably. If the situation at the outset is one of macroeconomic equilibrium, trade liberalization should lead to—or require—depreciation of the exchange rate, which will restore equilibrium. This "compensatory" devaluation, by increasing the value of imports in local currency, would mitigate the potential loss of receipts due to tax abatement. Some countries of the region (such as Chile between 1983 and 1988 and Colombia in the late 1980s) pursued an active exchange policy aimed at promoting greater competitiveness of national production. Others had to implement exchange adjustments prior to liberalization to restore external equilibrium and to generate a trade surplus large enough to cover the financial transfers abroad required by the debt crisis. In some cases, however, priority was given to the stabilization policy, the nominal exchange rate was fixed and, as a result, appreciation of the local currency was permitted (Argentina and Chile 1976-81 and Mexico from 1987 on).

---

[32] Thus, for example, the World Bank (1991a) noted that the loss of customs receipts due to trade liberalization was severe in Kenya, the Philippines, and Zaire, and that in some cases, such as Morocco and Thailand, the lowering of tariffs had to be reversed. Mitra (1990) has shown that this problem greatly impeded the trade liberalization process in other Asian countries such as India and Bangladesh.

The response of imports also depends on the effects that trade liberalization, exchange adjustments and the handling of other economic policy tools (stabilization programs in particular) have on the pace of economic activity, as well as the income elasticity of imports.

In the long term, if the liberalization process culminates in very low real tariffs, the effect on customs receipts will almost surely be negative. In the final analysis, in developed countries with more open economies and very low tariffs, customs receipts are practically negligible. The tax structures typically evolve from an initial heavy reliance on taxes on foreign trade to growing dependence on general taxes on domestic business activity (direct taxes and VAT or sales tax), as the process of development and economic modernization progresses.

Export Taxes

One of the objectives of trade liberalization is to eliminate the biases against exports that are generally an adjunct of protectionist policies. Consequently, liberalization processes usually eliminate or reduce direct export taxes. Economic theory admits of only two exceptions: cases in which domestic supply affects international prices and those in which taxes are used to stabilize the receipts from commodities exports.

Three of the four countries studied have used various types of export taxes. Argentina frequently used them, initially to compensate for the difficulty of imposing direct taxes on the agriculture and livestock export sector and, especially in the 1980s, as a simple expedient for dealing with fiscal crises, given the political difficulties facing basic tax reforms. This expedient was always temporary, however, because of fluctuations in the real exchange rate, and when the local currency appreciated, it became necessary to lower the export taxes. In recent years progress has been made toward eliminating them entirely.

In Colombia, taxes on coffee exports go partly to the FNC and partly to the national government. The part received by the government was initially justified in much the same way as the export taxes in Argentina (a way of taxing coffee growers, given the difficulty of controlling direct taxes) and has been gradually decreasing since 1976. The part that goes to the National Coffee Fund constitutes a portion of the income that the Fund uses to fulfill its function of stabilizing coffee receipts.[33]

In Mexico, taxes on petroleum and natural gas exports have provided a

---

[33] The Fund also makes physical and social infrastructure expenditures in the coffee-growing regions, fulfilling some of the government's functions in these regions.

means of transferring some of PEMEX's petroleum surplus to the central government. For this reason they are not, strictly speaking, taxes on foreign trade.

Taxes on Foreign Trade vs. Domestic Taxes

In cases where liberalization causes a significant loss of short-term customs receipts, the liberalization process can lead to fiscal disequilibrium if compensatory measures are not adopted.[34] Some authors have suggested that the most logical compensatory mechanism in these cases is increasing the VAT (or the general sales tax) (see Mitra, 1990).

In fact, import levies have historically had two objectives: protection and tax revenue. The purpose of trade liberalization and tax abatement, on the other hand, is to reduce the level of protection and expose domestic activities to greater competition, and not to sacrifice government resources.

Economic theory suggests that the objectives of protection and revenue should be attained by other means: protection through tariffs, and tax revenue through sales taxes or the VAT, which make no distinction between imported and domestic goods and services. The total tax receipts obtained through import levies is the sum of these two taxes. Consequently, if tariffs are lowered to decrease the level of protection, the rate of the VAT (or of the sales tax) should be increased accordingly to avoid a decrease in tax receipts.

The adjustment does not have to be proportional since the rate of the VAT (or of the sales tax) affects all domestic consumption as well as imports and is applied to the price of imports, which includes the tariff.[35] Moreover, for purely fiscal reasons, the tariff structure frequently includes very high tariffs for goods not produced domestically (such as luxury goods). In these cases, the levy may become an excise tax, either through a differential rate category in the VAT or as a specific additional tax. This means, of course, that it is essential to harmonize tariff reform and fiscal reform, as is well known but not widely practiced (Rajaram, 1991; World Bank, 1991a).[36]

The above reference to the smaller countries of the region warrants comment. In such cases it may be very difficult to shift the tax burden from foreign

---

[34] Various studies have warned of this danger, with the result, as Halevi (1989) states, that in organizations such as the World Bank "It is now a generally accepted fact that trade liberalization can be delayed or derailed by the lack of complementary macroeconomic policies and, in particular, appropriate fiscal policies." The same situation is warned of in other publications of the World Bank (Mitra, 1990) and the IMF (Farhadian-Lorie and Katz, 1989, and Blejer and Cheasty, 1988).

[35] Moreover, an exact, product-for-product compensation is not the objective, but rather a reproduction of the existing tariff dispersion in the structure of VAT (or sales tax) rates.

[36] In the latter publication, it is noted that the Bank at first assumed that trade liberalization would expand the tax base in such a way as to compensate for the effect of lowering tariffs, but this was not the case. Consequently, for some time now, the Bank has been recommending explicit compensatory measures in domestic taxes.

trade to the VAT or to general income taxes. In extreme cases, it is possible to imagine situations in which the VAT and the tariff are virtually the same thing but with a different name (e.g., a country that exports a natural resource and imports all of its consumer goods). Without going to this extreme, in most countries of the region a very significant percentage of the VAT receipts comes from imports, and the proportion is much greater than it would be if there were no control difficulties.

In fact, consideration of control difficulties and, consequently, the collection costs (both those incurred by the government [enforcement costs] and by individuals [compliance costs]) can change the conclusions of economic theory about what an "optimal" tax system is and, in particular, about the superiority of the VAT as opposed to tariffs (Shah and Slemrod, 1990).[37] By incorporating growing cost factors, economic theory concludes that the optimal mix contains some VAT and some tariffs, the proportions depending on the base of domestic production and the costs of levying taxes on it (Mihaljek, 1992). This result is even more pronounced if certain practical limitations of the VAT (such as its customary legal exclusion from the primary sectors and its de facto exclusion from the informal sectors) are taken into account, as a result of which its net effect on the efficiency of resource allocation differs considerably from the theoretical model.

Trade liberalization itself has indirect effects on other taxes, determined by the response of the competitive sectors to imports and economic activity in general, as well as the specific characteristics of each tax system. These effects tend to be negative in the short term because of the probable, initially recessive impact of liberalization, and even if they are positive they will scarcely compensate for a significant loss of customs receipts. Furthermore, even though liberalization affects economic activity and other variables that impact significantly on public finances (real exchange rate, inflation rate, interest rate), the latter generally depend more on other factors (prior macroeconomic imbalances, external shocks).

In the medium or long term it is likely that trade liberalization, as some authors (Tanzi, 1989) maintain, will have a net positive impact not only on other taxes in real terms but even on the overall tax burden (measured as a percentage of GDP) due to its potential effects on the efficiency of the economy, on the growth of the sectors that produce tradable goods and services and on the modernization process. Such a result, however, would take time, would be influenced by many other factors in addition to trade liberalization and could possibly require deliberate decisions aimed at expanding the base of the taxes on domestic activity and at improving their design and administration.

---

[37] The World Bank's *Report on World Development 1988* calculates the administrative costs of the taxes on trade and consumption at 1 percent to 3 percent of the total receipts, the VAT at 5 percent and income tax at 10 percent.

The Evidence

National Experiences

Chile. Between 1974 and 1980, nominal tariffs in Chile were gradually reduced (and their initially wide dispersion gradually eliminated), from an annual average of 105 percent in 1973 to a uniform 10 percent between 1980 and 1982.

At the start of the process, in late 1973 and 1974, tariff exemptions were eliminated—even for the public sector—and quasi-tariff restrictions were replaced with tariffs. Thus, despite a decrease in the nominal average from 105 to 49 percent between 1972 and 1974, the average real tariff fell from close to 15.6 percent in 1972 to 13.9 percent in 1975, after increasing in 1974 (Meller, 1992).[38] In the following years, the average real tariff decreased following the reduction in the nominal average, although gradually thanks to the effect of the smaller dispersion of the tariffs and the change in the composition of imports. Thus, although the nominal average fell 86.7 percent between 1974 and 1980, the real average decreased only 65.7 percent and even increased slightly between 1979 and 1981. Comparing the figures for 1982 and 1972 (one of the most representative years of the period prior to liberalization in 1973) shows that while the average tariff is barely 9.5 percent of the initial figure, the real tariff is 42.7 percent. The effect of eliminating exemptions and the dispersion of the tariffs therefore went a long way towards compensating for the loss of receipts that lowering the nominal tariffs would have caused.

Table 3.1 summarizes the trend of customs receipts in various periods and the contribution of changes in the real tariff, the real exchange rate and the import/GDP ratio (in real terms) to that trend.[39] As indicated in the table (1975 figures compared to 1972 figures), customs receipts in the first stage of liberalization rose from 1.6 percent to 2.9 percent of GDP as a result of devaluation, the fact that the elimination of exemptions largely neutralized the effect of the reduction of nominal tariffs (so that the real tariff decreased very little), and the fact that the lifting of import restrictions made it possible to maintain the real imports/GDP ratio despite its relative increase.

From 1975 to 1981, the positive effect of the considerable increase in the import ratio was not sufficient to offset the effects of the reduction of nominal tariffs (moderated by the reduction of their dispersion and the changes in the composition of imports) and appreciation of the real exchange rate. Even so,

---

[38] The 1973 and 1974 figures (for both receipts and the real tariff) differ enormously from one source to another (IMF, Meller, Larrain, Corbo). For this reason, and because 1973 was in any case an extremely atypical year, these two years are not included in this analysis.

[39] This is a linear decomposition exercise; consequently, the results are not exact and become even less so as the variations increase in size.

Table 3.1 Liberalization and Customs Receipts
(Percentage of GDP)

CHILE

	1972	1976	1981	1985	1990		75-72	81-75	91-85	95-90
Customs receipts/GDP	1.6	2.9	1.7	3.0	2.8	Customs receipts/GDP variation	1.3	-1.3	1.3	-0.2
Real tariff						A. Source: Meller				
A. Source: Meller	15.6	13.9	8.6	17.1	n.a.	Contr. of the real tariff	-0.2	-0.9	1.2	n.a.
B. Source: IMF	n.a.	16.5	10.1	23.1	13.6	Contr. of the exchange rate	1.9	-0.5	1.6	n.a.
Exchange rate[1]	50.8	124.3	92.2	205.6	195.1	Contr. of the import ratio[2]	-0.0	1.1	-1.0	n.a.
Import ratio[1]	43.1	44.5	107.6	45.8	97.8	(Explained variation)	1.7	-0.2	1.9	n.a.
						B. Source: IMF				
						Contr. of the real tariff	n.a.	-0.9	1.4	-1.4
						Contr. of the exchange rate	n.a.	-0.5	1.6	-0.1
						Contr. of the import ratio[2]	n.a.	1.1	-1.0	1.3
						(Explained variation)	n.a.	-0.3	2.0	-0.2

ARGENTINA

	1975	1981	1984	1987	1989		81-75	84-81	87-84	89-87
Customs receipts/GDP	0.83	1.40	0.6	1.25	0.50	Customs receipts/GDP variation	0.6	-0.8	0.6	-0.7
Real tariff	13.8	27.8	21.7	29.2	18.2	Contr. of the real tariff	0.9	-0.2	0.2	-0.4
Exchange rate[1]	280.3	129.3	265.9	271.6	415.1	Contr. of the exchange rate	-0.6	1.8	0.0	0.5
Import ratio[1]	59.9	81.1	37.3	48.8	32.4	Contr. of the import ratio[2]	0.6	-0.8	0.3	-0.3
						(Explained variation)	0.9	0.8	0.5	-0.2

(Cont.)

Table 3.1 (cont.)

MEXICO

	1976	1984	1987	1988		84-80	87-84	88-87
Customs receipts/GDP	1.15	0.45	0.87	0.6	Customs receipts/GDP variation	-0.7	0.4	-0.3
Real tariff	1.48	11.7	15.1	7.3	Contribution of the real tariff	-0.1	0.1	-0.5
Exchange rate[1]	100.0	136.8	179.2	143.6	Contribution of the exchange rate	0.5	0.2	-0.2
Import ratio[1]	100.0	50.7	66.6	82.8	Contribution of the import ratio[2]	-0.6	0.0	0.4
					(Explained variation)	-0.1	0.4	-0.2

COLOMBIA

	1975	1978	1984	1986	1989		78-75	84-78	86-84	89-86
Customs receipts/GDP	1.3	1.5	1.2	1.9	2.1	Customs receipts/GDP variation	0.2	-0.3	0.8	0.2
Real tariff	15.8	16.6	16.3	33.3	29.6	Contr. of the real tariff	0.1	0.0	1.2	-0.3
Exchange rate[1]	120.9	100.2	84.8	144.6	164.8	Contr. of the exchange rate	-0.2	-0.2	0.9	0.3
Import ratio[1]	52.9	78.2	80.1	70.1	83.9	Contr. of the import ratio[2]	0.3	-0.2	-0.3	0.1
						(Explained variation)	0.2	-0.4	1.7	0.2

[1] Base 1980 = 100.
[2] Estimated by the variation in imports less the variation in GDP.
Source: Case studies.

the loss of receipts was scarcely comparable to the initial gain, so that by 1981 they were 1.68 percent of GDP, slightly higher than the 1972 figure.[40]

It should also be noted that in 1975, replacement of the sales tax with a VAT with a higher equivalent rate generated an increase in total import taxes during the period.

After the crisis of 1982, Chile followed a policy of constant real devaluation (with a view to completing the productive structural reform undertaken with trade liberalization) and, in response to the fiscal crisis, raised the nominal tariffs to 20 percent in 1983 and to 25 percent in 1984 (reaching a one-time maximum of 35 percent) and then reduced them again to 20 percent in 1986 and to 15 percent in 1988 as the improvement in copper prices and the fiscal effects of devaluation permitted. The increase in the real tariff and devaluation caused a substantial rise in customs receipts (equivalent to 1.3 percent of GDP from 1981 to 1985), despite the decrease in the import ratio. Its subsequent reduction and, to a lesser extent, exchange appreciation, wiped out most of this gain (Table 3.1).

From 1982 to 1988 the impact of real devaluation on VAT receipts was greater than on customs receipts (Table 1.5) since the basic VAT rate was higher than the average tariff for most of this period and it was applied to the CIF value of imports plus the tariff.[41] This fact illustrates the importance of the introduction of a high VAT at the start of the trade liberalization and tariff reduction process in 1975; compensatory exchange adjustments (or those carried out in response to external shocks) and the growth of imports generated larger revenues from the VAT on imports during periods when the lowering of tariffs had a negative effect on customs receipts (1975-81 and from 1985 on).

Argentina. In the first phase of the trade liberalization process in Argentina (1976-81), the weighted average tariff fell from 94 to 53 percent in December 1977 (with a fluctuation band ranging from 10 percent for non-local inputs to 100 percent for certain consumer goods), and it continued falling in the second phase (from 1979 to 1981). Nevertheless, there was an upturn in the average real tariff (which contributed 0.4 percent of GDP to the increase in customs re-

---

[40] Trade liberalization and exchange management also affected the pace of economic activity and the transformation of its structure, trend of domestic interest rates, the inflation rate and other economic variables which, in turn, affected public finances. Nevertheless, the external shocks during this period and other policy instruments had as much or more of an impact than market deregulation on the trend of these variables, exchange management and public finances themselves. In particular, variations in copper prices and the debt crisis had substantial effects—both direct and indirect—on the trend of public finances. The quantification and separation of these effects, however, would require the use of macroeconomic or general equilibrium models beyond the scope of this study. Even so, it does not appear that the indirect effects of liberalization and exchange management on public finances were greater than the more direct effects mentioned above.

[41] This effect compensated for most of the deterioration of the VAT on domestic business activity between 1983 and 1987.

ceipts between 1975 and 1981). This was due to the elimination of the ban on the importation of goods subject to the highest tariffs, the initial replacement of some non-tariff restrictions with tariffs and a change in the composition of imports since, with liberalization and economic recovery, durable consumer goods grew fastest and were subject to the highest taxes.

The increase in the average real tariff and, in particular, the considerable rise in the import ratio had a combined effect on customs receipts which greatly exceeded the negative effect of the substantial exchange rate appreciation; as a result, customs receipts grew approximately 0.6 percent of GDP in the period.

In the following period (1981-84), exactly the opposite occurred. The economic crisis, the reimposition of non-tariff restrictions and devaluation caused imports to contract and changed their composition to the reverse of what it had been in the liberalization phase, with the result that the average real tariff was considerably reduced. These two effects neutralized the impact of devaluation on receipts, so that receipts decreased 0.8 percent of GDP.[42] Subsequently (1984-87), there was another surge in receipts, due entirely to the effect of the across-the-board increase in nominal tariffs carried out in conjunction with the Austral Plan in 1985.

In the second liberalization phase, the average real tariff was reduced (from 12 percent in late 1988 to 5.1 percent in late 1991), although less than the nominal tariffs (the ratio of nominal to average real tariffs decreased from 1.97 to 1.64 during this period and hit its lowest point [1.38] in early 1991), owing to the smaller dispersion of the tariffs, the change in the composition of imports (again involving increased imports of consumer goods) and, to a certain extent, improvements in the customs administration (World Bank, 1992b). The reduction of the average real tariff and exchange appreciation caused a significant drop in receipts (from 1.3 percent of GDP in 1987 to 0.3 percent in 1990 and 0.4 percent in 1991), despite the increase in the import ratio. This decrease, however, was ultimately offset by increased VAT receipts starting in 1990.[43]

Likewise, the reduction of the taxes on traditional exports in the first liberalization phase (from 36 percent to 3 percent as a simple average) and the revaluation of the currency caused a decrease in these receipts from 1.5 percent of GDP in 1976 to 0.2 percent from 1979 to 1981.

In 1982, 1983, 1985 and 1989, export duties were increased for fiscal reasons (with a temporary reduction from 1986 to 1988). In the second liberalization phase nearly all the export taxes and duties were eliminated: in 1990 those on manufactured goods and in 1991 most of the ones affecting agricultural products, which in mid-1989 were taxed at rates of 20 percent and 30 percent,

---

[42] According to Carciofi (1990), the average real tariff went from 19.2 percent in 1980 to 9.2 percent in 1989.

[43] Receipts of which went from 3.7 percent of GDP in 1986-87 to 5.1 percent in 1991, after falling significantly until 1989.

respectively. In 1991 the 3 percent statistical tax and the 0.5 percent promotional tax were also eliminated. As a result of these cuts and exchange appreciation, receipts dropped from 1.6 percent of GDP in 1989 (2.2 percent in 1985) to 0.2 percent of GDP in 1991.

In short, the decrease in the taxes on foreign trade was approximately 2.6 percent of GDP from 1985 to 1991. This reduction was, however, partially offset with increases in VAT receipts starting in 1991.

Mexico.   Prior to June 1985, 92.2 percent of all Mexican imports required licenses. The easing of controls that year lowered licensing to 47.1 percent. This percentage kept falling, to 35.8 percent in June 1987, to 25.4 percent in December 1987 and to 22.3 percent in March 1989 (Oks, 1992). The lowering of tariffs also began in 1985, reducing dispersion[44] and replacing non-tariff restrictions with tariffs on the eve of Mexico's accession to the GATT in 1986. The weighted nominal average was 22.8 percent in April 1980 and rose to 23.5 percent in June 1985 and to 28.5 percent in December 1985 as a result of the initial replacement of non-tariff restrictions with tariffs. The reduction of the average tariff began in June 1986 (24 percent) and June 1987 (22.7 percent), but the smaller dispersion and the change in the composition of imports caused an upturn in the average tariff until 1987.

Table 3.1 shows that from 1984 to 1987 the effect of devaluation and the increase in the average real tariff permitted a rise of 0.4 percent of GDP in customs receipts. The import ratio did not decrease in this period because the effects of liberalization counteracted the impact of the recession and the devaluation of 1986.

The largest tariff reductions began in December 1987. In recent years, the average tariff has varied between 11 percent and 12.6 percent. In addition, dispersion has been continually reduced. In 1988, the lowering of real tariffs closely followed that of the nominal tariffs and, together with exchange appreciation, caused a decrease of 0.8 percent of GDP in customs receipts, despite the increase in the import ratio. As in Chile, the ultimate decrease in customs receipts was offset by an increase in the VAT on imports, equivalent to 0.6 percent of GDP between 1984 and 1989.

Colombia.   Prior to 1990, Colombia had used an elaborate series of bans, licenses and import quotas that was more stringent when foreign exchange was in short supply and less so in periods of plenty (coffee booms) and during some unsuccessful episodes of gradual and partial trade liberalization and tax relief. In these episodes, typically, the slight lowering of tariffs was wholly or par-

---

[44]The maximum tariff was 100 percent until December 1985. It was reduced to 45 percent in June 1986, to 40 percent in June 1987 and to 20 percent in December 1987.

tially offset by the change in the composition of imports, so that the average real tariff changed very little. The variations in receipts were determined by the degree of exchange appreciation generally accompanying liberalization processes and the response of imports. The last of these episodes occurred between 1977 and 1983 (Table 3.1): a slight rise in the real tariff and an increase in the import ratio compensated for most of the negative effect of exchange appreciation on customs receipts.

The subsequent fiscal adjustment of 1985-86 was based in part on an increase in tariffs and other import taxes (a general surcharge that was raised to 18 percent) and on the fiscal effects of devaluation (see Chapter One).

In 1990 an aggressive trade liberalization and tax abatement process was initiated, originally intended to last four years. Its ultimate goals were reached in early 1991, however, despite the failure of the stabilization program then in progress and the lack of an initial response from imports.[45] The result was the most accelerated liberalization and tax abatement process set in motion in the hemisphere.

The proportion of tariff items requiring a license was over 80 percent in 1985 and 1986, 61 percent in 1989 and only 3 percent in late 1990, barely covering agricultural products. Then, in 1991, the license for major agricultural imports was replaced by a variable tariff, determined by the level of international prices.

The average tariff, on the other hand, dropped from 27 percent to 21 percent in 1990 and to 7 percent in 1991, while the general surcharge on imports decreased from 18 percent to 13 percent in 1990 and to 5 percent in 1991. Thus, the total fell from 44.6 percent in late 1989 to 33.3 percent in 1990 and to 11.9 percent in 1991. In addition, dispersion was drastically reduced. In 1992, trade with Venezuela was completely deregulated and exempted from taxes and a common external tariff was agreed upon, the average of which (tariff plus surcharge) is approximately 11 percent. Other countries in the Andean Group subsequently acceded to this agreement.

In 1990 an effort was made to compensate for the expected loss of customs receipts by raising the rate of the VAT from 10 percent to 12 percent. The additional losses ensuing from the decisions of 1991 were estimated by the IMF as the equivalent of 0.2 percent of GDP in 1991, 0.9 percent in 1992, 0.5 percent in 1993 and 0.4 percent in 1994 and 1995.[46] These estimates assume a dynamic response from imports starting in 1992 (which, in fact, is happening)

---

[45] The acceleration of the inflationary process was primarily a result of the exchange management, but the authorities tried to stop it with a very strict fiscal and monetary policy. The result was a considerable hike in interest rates, the slowing of economic activity and, most importantly, a sharp decrease in investment. The resulting drop in capital goods imports more than compensated for the increase in imports of consumer goods.

[46] The government's estimates are somewhat higher (1.1 percent of GDP in 1992 and 1993).

and also that the authorities would be able to avoid sharp appreciation of the peso, which has not happened.

The government proposed compensating for this loss by raising the VAT from 12 percent to 18 percent,[47] but Congress only authorized an increase to 14 percent and opted for a temporary surcharge (five years) on income tax that was higher than the one proposed by the government, reversing the orientation of the 1986 tax reform.

In short, liberalization neutralized part of the fiscal adjustment of 1985-86 and forced the government to raise the basic VAT and income taxes, thereby changing the focus of the tax policy of that period. In retrospect, it would have been better had the fiscal adjustment of 1985-86 been based on the reinforcement of basic taxes and not the taxes on foreign trade.[48]

Conclusions

The characteristics of the protective structure and the method and sequence of liberalization were such that in three of the cases studied customs receipts remained constant or increased at the start of the liberalization and tax abatement process. In fact, the elimination of exemptions (Chile, 1974-75), the replacement of non-tariff restrictions with tariffs (Mexico 1985) and the increase in imports subject to the highest tariffs following the lifting of quantitative restrictions (Argentina, 1976-81) led to an initial rise in the average real tariff. This, together with the effect of the initial devaluation, boosted customs receipts (as a percentage of GDP) in these three countries in the early stages of the liberalization process.

In Colombia, however, trade liberalization from 1990 on led to a significant loss of customs receipts in the short term. There were several reasons for this:
• The adjustment initiated in 1985 was based—as indicated above—largely on higher import taxes and the fiscal impact of an aggressive real devaluation process, originally intended to reduce the external deficit and then to prepare the economy for liberalization. Both factors, in addition to the effect of the gradual easing of import restrictions, caused a substantial increase in the ratio of customs receipts to GDP (from 1.2 percent in 1984 to 2.1 percent in 1989).
• Although trade liberalization began with the elimination of non-tariff restrictions such as permit requirements in 1990, the latter were basically redundant since Colombia had always used the permit system to achieve short-term

---

[47] Intended in part to allow credit for the VAT paid on purchases of capital goods, changing from an income type VAT to a consumption type.
[48] Which would have required a smaller reduction in the income tax rates than those that occurred in this period.

equilibrium and, consequently, relaxed its enforcement when foreign exchange was plentiful. Furthermore, the recession of 1991 caused the contraction of imports. In these circumstances, the most significant effects were the rapid reduction of tariffs in 1991, which lowered the average nominal tariff from 43 percent to 12 percent and reduced the dispersion of tariffs, and the appreciation of the exchange rate as a result of the considerable inflow of capital that year.

The recent trade liberalization program in Argentina also led to a significant loss of receipts (from 1.7 percent in 1987 to 0.3 percent in 1990). The rapid lowering of tariffs and the appreciation permitted because of the priority assigned stabilization objectives in exchange management offset the impact of expanded imports. This result was reinforced by the elimination of export taxes, which had been a preferred means of managing fiscal crises in the 1980s.

Despite these differences in the short-term trend of receipts, the experiences studied leave little doubt about the direction of the long-term effects. In both Chile and Mexico, the initial rise in customs receipts followed a period of steady decline (in Chile from 1976 to 1981; in Mexico from 1988 on). At the same time, the nominal reduction of tariffs neutralized the initial impact of the elimination of exemptions and non-tariff restrictions, and a process of appreciation for stabilization purposes counteracted the effects of the initial devaluation.

In all the countries studied, potential decreases in customs receipts were offset wholly or in part by increases in the VAT. In Chile, the VAT was introduced at the start of the liberalization period (1975), and the increased revenue it generated compensated for losses in customs receipts from 1976 to 1981. The same thing happened in Argentina during this period. In more recent liberalization processes, VAT receipts also increased as customs receipts dwindled. In contrast to previous experiences, however, the VAT was adjusted after the loss of customs receipts had already begun. In some countries, such as Colombia, this was the express purpose of the VAT reform. Usually, however, the adjustment was prompted by more general aspects of the fiscal situation.

CHAPTER FOUR

REFORM OF THE STATE
AND PUBLIC FINANCES

The Fiscal Impact of Decentralization

The difficulty of fiscal adjustment in various Latin American countries cannot be understood without considering the structure of intergovernmental finances. This is especially true of two of the countries covered by this study—Argentina and Colombia.

The most sensitive and most significant topic in this respect concerns the finances of the territorial entities and their share of the revenue collected by the national government. The importance of this topic depends on the type of government (federal or central) and how aggressively the policy of decentralizing government activities is being pursued.

In federal states there is considerable pressure to apportion functions and resources. States or provinces tend to act with a certain degree of fiscal irresponsibility; and since the federal government has no adequate means of control, the overall management of public finances becomes very complicated. In other instances, however, the federal government seeks to balance its finances by "exporting" the problem to the provinces. Both problems are clearly illustrated in the section on Argentina.

In countries with non-federated states, recent decentralization processes have been prompted by considerations of efficiency, local control and the functioning of the democratic process. Independent of their results vis-a-vis these objectives, which are not the subject of this study, decentralization processes create problems for the management of public finances, as the section on Colombia amply demonstrates.

First, in some cases, the question arises as to what extent the division or transfer of responsibilities and resources between the central (or federal) government and the territorial entities complicates the attainment of overall equilibrium in public finances and, more particularly, how it contributed to the fiscal difficulties of the 1980s.

Second, experience has shown that the taxes with the largest base and highest fiscal yield (income tax, the VAT, and taxes on foreign trade) must be administered by the central or federal government because of their technical characteristics. Mexico's experience with decentralized administration of the VAT is proof of this assertion. It is therefore essential that mechanisms be established to transfer resources from the national treasury to the territorial entities. The dissimilarity of the fiscal capabilities of the regional and local entities reinforces this need.

When the central authorities have discretionary power over the amounts to be distributed and the rules for their distribution, the planning and management of state activities assigned to regional and local entities becomes extremely unstable and uncertain, thus eliminating the potential advantages of decentralization. Moreover, constant political strife ensues, and this exhausts officials at all levels and makes the flow and distribution of resources even more unpredictable.

Consequently, many countries have established automatic mechanisms to transfer and distribute national resources. The design of these mechanisms, however, poses a number of problems.

• Frequently, the transfer or "share" is based on the proceeds of specific central government revenue items. This creates serious biases in the management of tax policy, since the central authorities tend to prefer "unshared " taxes (or other revenues), even though they are not the most efficient. Argentina's experience is a good example of this problem, which has been satisfactorily resolved in Colombia.

• Ideally, resources should be distributed among the recipient entities on the basis of the spending requirements they cannot meet with their own revenue-generating capacity. The actual rules do not adhere to this principle and, more particularly, do not encourage individual tax efforts. In these conditions, the elasticity of aggregate fiscal revenues, as compared to national revenues, tends to deteriorate and the reliance of territorial finances on central government transfers increases, placing an excessive burden on the finances of the central administration.

The Argentine Experience

In 1983 the consolidated deficit of the nonfinancial public sector was generated almost equally by the national government, the provinces, and public enterprises.[49] Nevertheless, the tax effort launched that same year devolved on the national government, followed—with some delay—by the public enterprises and then the provinces, which made only a slight contribution (Tables 4.1 and 4.2).[50]

In 1987 the deficit in provincial finances was more than twice as large as it was in 1977, and despite the central government's efforts to increase and standardize funds transfers and to cut off the provinces' access to sources of deficit financing from then on, the deficit kept growing until the end of the decade and then decreased very slightly in mid-1991.

The fiscal deficits of the provinces and public enterprises were financed largely with transfers from the national government, which grew to more than 10 percent of GDP in 1975 and 1983-89 (peaking at 13.8 percent in 1983). Consequently, the national government, despite generating its own surplus since 1984, experienced financing shortfalls in excess of 3 percent of GDP every year from 1973 to 1990,[51] which largely explains the economic instability of the decade (see the section in Chapter Two entitled "Consequences of a Prolonged Fiscal Deficit: Overindebtedness ").

Financing the provinces has wrought enormous fiscal and political havoc since 1980. That year's tax reform, by using some of the VAT to finance social security, led to a reduction in the distribution rate of the so-called "shared taxes," which went from 50.5 percent to 26.9 percent in 1981-82, to 21.5 percent in 1983 and to 24.4 percent in 1984. In 1984, the Federal Revenue Sharing Law, which governed the transfers, expired and was not replaced with an

---

[49] The deficit generated at each level is defined as the deficit less transfers to and from other levels of government.

[50] The finances of the national government (central administration, special accounts and decentralized entities) went from a position of virtual equilibrium in 1977 —before the transfers were established— to a deficit of approximately 6 percent of GDP in 1982, and then to a surplus of about 2 percent of GDP in 1985 and 1986. The fiscal austerity of the national government can be seen more clearly in the primary balance it generated, which had included a surplus since 1977 (peaking at 5.2 percent to 9.6 percent of GDP, depending on the source, in 1985).

The deficit generated in the provinces (which is almost entirely a primary deficit) rose from 1.3 percent of GDP in 1977 to 5.3 percent of GDP in 1984 (with a temporary reduction in 1982), and then fell to levels close to 3 percent of GDP between 1985 and 1987. In 1989 a slight improvement was observed.

As far as the public enterprises are concerned, the ordinary deficit (about half of which is a primary deficit) grew to 7 percent of GDP in 1982 (from 2.8 percent of GDP in 1977) and then fell to 2.3 percent in 1986. The deficit increased again until 1988 (4 percent of GDP) and then decreased considerably in 1990 as a result of the drastic cuts in their investments and the privatization of public enterprises which showed a deficit. Social security showed a small cash surplus until 1985; after that it showed a deficit (primary) of approximately 1 percent GDP.

[51] The financing shortfalls reached 12.4 percent in 1979 and 16.5 percent in 1983.

Table 4.1 Surplus (Deficit) Generated at Each Government Level
(Percentage of GDP)

	Colombia					Argentina				
	1980	1983	1984	1985	1990	1977	1982	1983	1984	1987
I. Nation										
Own surplus (deficit)	5.3	4.2	3.4	4.9	5.6	-0.7	-6.1	-4.0	-1.8	-0.0
Own primary surplus (deficit)	5.8	4.9	4.3	5.9	7.0	0.5	0.1	-0.7	1.2	1.9
II. National decentralized entities[1]										
Own surplus (deficit)	-0.9	-0.9	0.0	0.4	-1.9	0.0	0.0	0.1	0.0	-0.9
Own primary surplus (deficit)	-0.9	-0.4	0.5	0.7	-0.7	0.0	0.0	0.1	0.0	-0.9
III. National public enterprises										
Own surplus (deficit)	-1.8	-3.1	-1.6	-2.8	1.9	-2.8	-6.9	-6.3	-4.9	-3.3
Own primary surplus (deficit)	-1.1	-2.4	-0.8	-1.6	3.3	-1.9	-2.8	-3.8	-2.9	-1.6
IV. Provinces[2]										
Own surplus (deficit)	-1.2	-3.4	-3.0	-2.9	-4.4	-1.3	-2.2	-4.9	-5.3	-3.0
Own primary surplus (deficit)	-0.9	-2.9	-2.4	-2.1	-3.4	-1.3	-2.0	4.7	-5.3	-2.9

[1] Social security figures in Argentina.
[2] Includes the departments and municipalities in Colombia and the provinces and the municipality of the City of Buenos Aires in Argentina.
Source: Case studies.

alternative legal system. In addition, the provinces were forced to increase their expenditures owing both to the transfer in 1977-80 of services formerly provided by the national government and to the contraction of their own resources in 1982 due to the economic crisis.

As a result, the automatic, legally-mandated contributions to the provinces were replaced by growing discretionary contributions. The disadvantages and constant conflicts caused by the discretionary allocation of resources to the provinces led to the passage of the Revenue Sharing Law (1988), which, like the previous law, required the automatic transfer of 57.7 percent of certain taxes (capital gains tax, minimum gross assets tax, the VAT and several minor taxes), total receipts of which represented 73 percent of the total estimated tax receipts in 1992.

Transfers to the provinces increased from 6.5 percent of GDP in 1983-85 to more than 7 percent in 1992, not only because the percentage established by the Revenue Sharing Law was the highest ever, but also because the growth of the most efficient taxes expanded the base of the shared taxes.[52]

In the mid-1980s, the Secretariat of Finance was directly responsible for only 20 percent of the total public spending, a fourth of which consisted of interest payments. At the same time, the federal government had assumed greater responsibility for providing resources, either through taxes or the central bank. When any of the decentralized entities, the provinces or the public enterprises encountered budgetary difficulties, they turned to the government or the central bank for ad-hoc solutions. Hyperinflation and economic instability, however, forced the Secretariat to concentrate on the management of short-term flows and not on the more basic aspects of intergovernmental finances and budgetary programming. In these circumstances, the strategy for controlling the expenses of other government levels was confined to limiting the access of the decentralized public sector to the treasury and the central bank. In 1987, an Investment Fund was set up using resources from enterprises with a surplus (YPF and communications) to pay the external debt of enterprises with a deficit. This fund was abolished in 1991.

These policies created distortions (due to cross subsidies between public enterprises) and the system ultimately failed because the entities found ways of satisfying their deficit financing requirements. Specifically, the provinces' deficits were financed by provincial banks, which then turned to the central bank; the Convertibility Law of 1992 blocked such access, but there was nothing to prevent the provincial banks from obtaining external credit (Barkai, 1992).

Furthermore, the provinces administered the industrial promotion system, which was one of the major reasons for the erosion of the bases of income, the VAT and import taxes in the 1980s.

---

[52] There were times, however, when the government increased the non-shared taxes more (1988 and 1990, for example).

Table 4.2. Nonfinancial Public Sector Operations by Government Level
(Percentages of GDP)

	Colombia					Argentina					
	1980	1983	1984	1985	1990	1977	1982	1983	1984	1987	1991
I. Nation											
Savings	5.8	4.5	3.6	5.2	5.8	4.0	-2.2	0.2	5.4	7.3	7.3
Current revenue	9.5	7.9	7.8	9.0	9.9	10.8	10.3	11.3	15.1	15.5	14.1
Current expenditures	2.9	3.4	4.1	3.8	4.1	6.8	12.5	11.1	9.7	8.2	6.8
Capital expenditures	0.3	0.3	0.2	0.3	0.2	3.7	2.6	2.9	1.6	1.7	1.4
Own surplus (deficit)	5.3	4.2	3.4	4.9	5.6	0.3	-4.8	-2.7	3.8	5.6	7.0
Net transfers	7.1	7.5	7.2	7.4	8.4	4.5	5.6	13.8	11.3	13.8	8.2
Financial surplus (deficit)	-1.8	-3.3	-3.8	-2.5	-0.8	-4.2	-10.4	-16.5	-7.5	-8.2	-1.2
II. National decentralized entities[1]											
Savings	1.2	1.3	1.6	1.8	-0.4	0.8	0.0	-0.9	-2.9	-1.0	-0.3
Current revenue	3.7	3.3	3.7	3.7	0.9	4.1	4.9	5.2	2.7	4.1	5.7
Current expenditures	2.5	2.0	1.9	1.9	1.3	3.3	4.9	6.1	5.6	5.1	6.0
Capital expenditures	2.2	2.2	1.8	1.4	1.4	0.7	0.0	0.0	0.0	0.0	0.0
Own surplus (deficit)	-0.9	-0.9	0.0	0.4	-1.9	0.1	0.0	-0.9	-2.9	-1.0	-0.3
Net transfers	1.1	1.0	1.0	1.0	1.3	0.0	0.0	0.0	-2.9	-0.9	0.0
Financial surplus (deficit)	-2.0	-1.9	-1.0	-0.6	-3.2	0.1	0.0	-0.9	0.0	-0.1	-0.3

Table 4.2. (cont.)

	Colombia					Argentina					
	1980	1983	1984	1985	1990	1977	1982	1983	1984	1987	1991
III. National public enterprises											
Savings	0.2	0.5	1.5	1.0	3.4	1.8	-3.9	-2.6	-1.5	0.2	-0.3
Current revenue	1.1	1.3	2.4	2.4	5.2	9.8	9.7	11.0	10.5	11.8	6.7
Current expenditures	0.9	0.8	0.9	1.4	1.8	8.0	13.6	13.6	12.0	11.6	7.0
Capital expenditures	2.1	3.5	3.1	3.8	1.4	4.9	3.4	3.9	3.8	3.6	0.0
Own surplus (deficit)	-1.8	-3.1	-1.8	-2.8	1.9	-2.7	-6.9	-6.3	-4.8	-3.3	-0.3
Net transfers	-1.0	-0.3	-0.4	0.3	1.4	-1.9	-1.9	-7.0	-3.0	-4.3	-0.8
Financial surplus (deficit)	-0.7	-2.7	-1.2	-3.1	0.5	-0.8	-5.0	0.7	-1.8	1.0	0.5
IV. Depts. and municipalities											
Savings	0.4	-0.7	-0.4	-0.2	-0.5	n.a.	n.a.	n.a.	n.a.	n.a.	n.a.
Current revenue	4.8	5.2	5.4	5.4	5.2	n.a.	n.a.	n.a.	n.a.	n.a.	n.a.
Current expenditures	4.3	5.9	5.8	5.6	5.7	n.a.	n.a.	n.a.	n.a.	n.a.	n.a.
Capital expenditures	1.9	2.9	2.9	2.9	4.3	n.a.	n.a.	n.a.	n.a.	n.a.	n.a.
Own surplus (deficit)	-1.2	-3.4	-3.0	-2.9	-4.4	n.a.	n.a.	n.a.	n.a.	n.a.	n.a.
Net transfers	-1.6	-2.6	-2.8	-2.3	-3.0	n.a.	n.a.	n.a.	n.a.	n.a.	n.a.
Financial surplus (deficit)	0.4	-0.8	-0.5	-0.5	-1.4	n.a.	n.a.	n.a.	n.a.	n.a.	n.a.

n.a. not available
[1] Social security figures in Argentina.
Source: Case studies.

Thus, the provinces requested ever larger transfers of funds from the federal government, while at the same time contributing to the contraction of its revenue. In these circumstances, the fiscal adjustment was necessarily limited to reducing the least politically sensitive expenditures: investments, wages and purchases of the central administration. In 1991, three-fourths of all federal outlays, excluding interest payments, were transfers to the provinces, public enterprises and the social security system.

In 1992 various initiatives were proposed to reduce the revenue sharing base and simultaneously facilitate the financing of programs with the largest net liabilities (social security and public housing) as well as to provide for a future reduction in payroll taxes, which are quite high in Argentina. Cutting payroll taxes, however, involves a sizable decrease in provincial financing, which could seriously complicate the management of provincial finances during recessions and prompt a return to the practice of making specific allocations, which had been on the decline in recent years.[53]

In fact, another manifestation of the problems of Argentina's fiscal structure is the enormous quantity of resources allocated through special accounts and funds, and through other mechanisms, resulting in reduced flexibility in the management of public finances. In 1989 there were 150 funds of this type; in 1990 the government took back 50 percent of their resources as an emergency solution, simplified the fuel tax structure and eliminated most of the complex intergovernmental transfers effected through special funds. In 1991 the number of special funds was reduced by a third, with plans to reduce them to 59 in 1992.

Much remains to be done in the system of intergovernmental finances and transfers to lend greater flexibility to public finances and increase the elasticity of public revenues. Specifically, the system of transfers to the provinces should include an incentive for the provinces to make their own tax effort and should be based on the nation's total revenues and not on certain specific taxes in order to avoid tax policy distortions caused by the varying degree of revenue sharing from one type of tax to another. The use of minor, inefficient taxes during fiscal crisis, which is a common practice in Argentina, was to some extent caused by this feature of the revenue sharing system. Finally, the government will have to regulate the access of provincial banks to credit; otherwise, it will be unable to ensure fiscal equilibrium in the provinces after the transfers are made.

---

[53] In June 1992, 11 percent of the total VAT receipts (the so-called social security VAT) was removed from the revenue sharing base and earmarked for social security. Later on, this percentage will be 15 percent. In addition, 40 percent of the fuel taxes was earmarked for government housing programs. The June 1992 bill proposed that 20 percent of the revenue from income tax and 36 percent of the VAT (40 percent in 1994) be allocated to social security starting in 1993.

The Colombian Experience

As was the case in Argentina, most of the fiscal adjustment effort in Colombia in the latter half of the 1980s was made by the national public sector, while the deficits of the departments and municipalities grew steadily throughout the decade, largely as a result of a deliberate policy of decentralizing public spending. Unlike Argentina, however, the adjustment originated more in the national public enterprises than in the central administration.

The deficit generated in the departments and municipalities grew 3.7 percent of GDP between 1980 and 1990, while finances at the central level deteriorated in the early 1990s and required a severe adjustment. The central administration's surplus shrank from 5.3 percent of GDP in 1980 to 3.4 percent in 1984 and then rebounded to figures of over 5.5 percent of GDP from 1986 on. The national public enterprises, on the other hand, increased their deficit in 1980-83 (from 1.8 percent of GDP to 3.1 percent of GDP) and ended the decade with a surplus of approximately 2 percent of GDP (Table 4.1).[54]

The growth of consolidated public spending in the first half of the 1980s and its subsequent reduction mask a profound change in the spending patterns at the various government levels. While the national government was making cuts in its total outlays, spending was on the rise in the departments (from 3.7 percent of GDP to 4.7 percent of GDP) and especially in the municipalities (from 2.5 percent of GDP to 5.4 percent of GDP). Of particular note was the change in the composition of public investments: while the capital expenditures of the municipalities rose from 1.2 percent of GDP to 3.1 percent of GDP and those of the departments increased from 0.7 percent of GDP to 1.1 percent of GDP, national sector capital expenditures decreased from 4.6 percent of GDP to 3 percent of GDP.

The slight reduction in operating expenses at the national level occurred entirely in the decentralized entities; in the central administration, these expenses increased (from 2.9 percent of GDP to 4.1 percent of GDP from 1980 to 1984, and then remained near this level). Consequently, social spending did not contract as it had in other Latin American countries.

Most of the cuts in investment at the national level were made by public enterprises (from 3.8 percent of GDP to 1.4 percent of GDP between 1985 and 1990), followed by the decentralized entities. At the same time, during the period when spending was on the rise (in the first half of the decade), the largest increase in investment occurred in the national public enterprises (from 2.1 percent of GDP to 3.8 percent of GDP).

---

[54] The balance of the national decentralized entities fluctuated between a deficit of 0.9 percent to 2.2 percent in the first four years of the decade and a surplus of 2.3 percent in 1986, followed by another deficit of 1.9 percent of GDP in 1990, in reaction to changes in the finances of the National Coffee Fund as the coffee-growing cycle progressed.

As indicated in Chapter One, these trends were due to the development of large energy and mining projects in the first half of the 1990s, so that the subsequent decline in investment was a natural consequence of the completion of these projects. Furthermore, the largest increase in current revenues at the national government level occurred in the national public enterprises (whose operating surplus swelled from 0.2 percent of GDP to 3.4 percent in 1990), due primarily to the subsequent yield of these investments. Much of the rise in the current revenue of the central and territorial administrations also came from larger oil and mining outputs.

The steady growth of the deficit in the departments and municipalities was covered with increasingly large transfers from the national budget. "Automatic" transfers to the territorial entities expanded from 14.4 percent of the current revenue of the national central administration in 1980 to 20.9 percent in 1986 and to 23.4 percent in 1990, in addition to the discretionary transfers, which by 1991 represented 7.5 percent of current revenues. This increase was largely offset, however, by a decrease in transfers to the national decentralized entities and public enterprises. Net transfers from the national central administration to the rest of the public sector rose from 4.7 percent of GDP in 1980 to 5.3 percent in 1984 and then fell to 4.4 percent in 1990. The work of the national government was primarily limited to establishing appropriate mechanisms for transferring resources from these enterprises to the national government (via legal changes that transferred royalties, income tax and corporate profit taxes) and decreasing transfers to the public entities in order to finance growing transfers to the departments and municipalities as well as the central administration's own deficit.

The decentralization process now underway cannot be understood apart from its historical background. Throughout the century, public sector current revenues and expenditure commitments have been concentrating in the national government (specifically, the national government's share of tax receipts went from 54 percent in 1930 to 84.5 percent in 1978). This process had a dual impact: on the one hand, the national government increased its share of total public expenditures and, on the other, departmental and municipal finances became increasingly dependent on transfers of funds from the central government.

Until 1967, these transfers were discretionary. The constitutional reform of 1968 established an automatic mechanism (the *situado fiscal*), equivalent to a certain percentage of the nation's "ordinary" revenues (current revenues not specifically allocated), to finance health and education in proportions established by law. Pursuant to Law 13 of 1968, a portion of the income tax receipts was transferred to the municipalities, and this amount was increased each time the tax was reformed.

The two systems for the automatic transfer of revenue from the national government represented 14.5 percent of the latter's revenues in 1980, 21 percent in 1986, close to 23 percent in 1991, and an estimated 25 percent in 1992. Thus, despite the fact that the national government increased its share of public sector current revenues (from 59.3 percent in 1967 to 66.4 percent in 1990), the receipts available to the central government (after the automatic transfers) decreased from 59.3 percent in 1967 to 48.1 percent in 1978 and then increased slightly to 51.6 percent in 1990. The surge in transfers (automatic transfers especially) to the departments and municipalities following the constitutional reform of 1968 more than compensated for the declining share of their own current revenues in the total collected by the public sector.

A critical subject from the viewpoint of overall public finances is whether this increase in unconditional transfers—automatic transfers in particular—discouraged the tax effort of the departments and municipalities. The nonborrowed revenue of both territorial entities decreased until the end of the 1970s, both as a percentage of GDP and as compared to total public sector revenues. These trends persisted in the 1980s in the departments, but not in the municipalities.[55] In particular, municipal tax receipts grew faster than national receipts (7.4 percent per annum in real terms, as compared to 3.9 percent in the national central sector and 2.9 percent in the departmental sector).

This change occurred after Law 14 of 1983 granted greater autonomy in taxation to the territorial entities, modernized and expanded their tax bases and shielded them against the negative effects of inflation. Later, Law 12 of 1986 made the major amounts transferred to the smaller municipalities conditional upon their own tax effort, and they were the quickest to increase their tax receipts.

In short, the departments made less and less of a tax effort, which can be attributed partly to the effect of the unconditional transfers of funds[56] and partly to the intrinsic inelasticity of departmental taxes. However, the evidence does not lead to the same conclusion with respect to the municipalities. It appears in this case that the decrease prior to 1983 was caused primarily by the lack of fiscal autonomy: the tax bases, tariffs and exemptions were all fixed by law or adjusted by the national government, which had no particular interest in increasing municipal receipts.

In addition to transfers to the territorial entities, the Colombian tax system, like that in Argentina, was characterized by a very large number of earmarked revenues (39 percent of the public current revenues in 1980, 54.2 percent in 1984 and 46 percent in 1987).[57]

Designed to provide greater flexibility, Law 55 of 1986 expanded the range

---

[55] Transfers from the national government were the equivalent of 75 percent of the departments' own revenues in 1980 and 103 percent in 1990. The corresponding percentages for the municipalities were 36.8 percent in 1980 and 73.7 percent in 1990.

[56] This is also related to the inelasticity of departmental taxes (liquor, beer, tobacco).

[57] This figure includes transfers to territorial entities, social security contributions and the profits retained by public enterprises (World Bank, 1992a).

of activities and entities that could be financed with a given earmarked re-source. In 1988, the enactment of a new budgetary law made the surpluses of public entities a part of the national budget and provided for the profits of pub-lic enterprises to be included as capital revenue in said budget.

The constitutional reform of 1991 introduced substantial changes, both in the system of transfers and in the earmarked revenues.

• Current revenues became the basis for determining both the transfer pay-ment and the contribution to the municipalities. The reason for this was to avoid biases in fiscal policy decisions and to prevent conflicts between the var-ious levels of government, given that the territorial entities receive a share of some taxes and not of others.
• The new constitution stipulated that the percentage of the transfer payment would increase gradually from the 1992 level to whatever amount was neces-sary to cover basic health and education needs, the functions of which were transferred in their entirety to the departments and municipalities. The per-centage of the contribution to the municipalities would increase gradually from 14 percent of current revenues in 1993 to a minimum of 22 percent within 10 years, as other functions of the national government are transferred to the municipalities.
• A new transfer mechanism was created using royalty income not committed to the producing departments and municipalities. These receipts would be dis-tributed among the territorial entities through a National Royalties Fund, the purpose of which is to finance regional projects and the costs of promoting mining activities and environmental protection.
• The reform eliminated and prohibited any earmarked revenues other than the three mentioned above, which are allocated to the territorial entities, and those used to cover social and environmental protection expenditures. In particular, this provision eliminates earmarking taxes on fuels, foreign trade, and many others.

As a result, total transfers to the territorial entities will increase from ap-proximately 32.7 percent of central government current revenues in 1992 (in-cluding 7.5 percent in discretionary transfers for health and education) to nearly 36.6 percent in 1993 and 47 percent in 2002.

These changes raise the following major concerns:

• Whether, as the constitution provides in principle, an equal transfer of re-sponsibilities and resources to the territorial entities is possible. The experi-ence of transferring resources and responsibilities under Law 12 of 1986 demonstrates the enormous difficulties involved.[58]

---

[58] For this reason, the authors of the constitution included a temporary article providing for a one-time reform, the proceeds of which would not be shared with the departments and municipalities,

• If these additional revenues are insufficient, how much of the difference can be made up with the reallocation of resources made possible by the elimination of other earmarked revenues?

• If the decentralization process requires additional revenues, what percentage will come from mounting petroleum tax receipts, as in the past,[59] and what percentage from a greater tax effort by the central administration or the departments and municipalities? The new constitution grants greater autonomy in taxation at the latter levels and stipulates that the criteria governing the distribution of transfers must include the tax effort, administrative efficiency and management results (in addition to the target population of the service, the tax effort and unmet basic needs). Its precise effect will depend, however, on the legal and administrative development of these standards.

Mexico's Experience with Decentralized Administration of the VAT

The introduction of the VAT in 1980 was a substantial improvement over the cumulative general sales tax and the nearly 300 specific, minor taxes it replaced. Nevertheless, since the latter were all taxes imposed by the states, administration of the VAT remained in their control. To boost receipts, a participatory arrangement was established to award the states for above-average collections. This, however, discouraged cooperation between the states, and since it was politically impossible to impose penalties for slow-growing receipts, the relative shares remained more or less the same and there was no incentive for additional collections (since the difference was ultimately split with 30 other states).

The slump in VAT receipts in the 1980s (the VAT on domestic activity slid from 2 percent of GDP in 1980 to 1.6 percent in 1982, rebounded to 2.3 percent in 1983—when the rate increased from 10 to 15 percent—and then fell again to 1.9 percent in 1989)[60] was essentially due to this administrative situation.[61]

To solve this problem, the participation arrangement was modified to allow the states to keep 30 percent of their individual receipts, beginning in 1987. The change represented a ninefold increase in the marginal revenue of each

---

in order to cover this potential difference. Consequently, the tax reform of 1992 provided that up to 3 percentage points of the general VAT rate in excess of 12 percent (currently 14 percent) and the "decentralization contribution" from the gasoline tax would go entirely to the national government (i.e., would not be included in the transfer payment or the allocation to the municipalities).

[59] New discoveries prior to the constitutional reform may make this possible, at least for a while.

[60] The portion collected in customs, however, went from 0.7 percent of GDP to 1.1 percent of GDP during the decade, partly as a result of the rise in the import ratio.

[61] A recent study estimates the loss due to administrative problems as 5.4 percent of the total VAT receipts. This figure is probably too low.

state, but its effect was never observed because the federal government took control of the VAT in 1988 and now administers it jointly with the income tax. The substantial rise in VAT receipts in recent years is related to this change.[62]

The Fiscal Impact of Privatization

Theory

Generally, the sale of any state asset has an initially positive impact on government cash flow and a subsequent negative impact, evinced by the net yields generated. The net effect can be appreciated by comparing the current value of the initial capital inflow with the subsequent loss of current revenues. The similarity to the effect of a credit on cash flow indicates that the sale of assets generally provides a means of financing a current deficit but not reducing it, as the fiscal records of most of the countries that follow the suggestions of the IMF in this regard unfortunately show.

This similarity also emphasizes the danger that the inflow of capital from the sale of assets will encourage the government to make excessive or imprudent expenditures and will enable it to circumvent fiscal discipline and adjustment, which is what happened with the capital obtained through foreign borrowing in the late 1970s. This danger increases when the government that receives the revenue is not the one that has to deal with the subsequent contraction. Moreover, the difference between a credit and the sale of an asset is that a credit generates increased current expenditures and not fewer receipts, and its cost is therefore more visible.

The privatization of state enterprises is somewhat different from the sale of other assets. First, the net effect on the flow of current revenues is more complex because the privatized enterprises will pay taxes. Nevertheless, if privatization does not generate a net increase in private investment but merely a change in its composition, crowding out other uses of funds available for investment, this effect will be offset by the taxes paid on the alternative investment. This consideration is omitted from the calculations usually made to estimate the fiscal impact of privatization (see below).

Moreover, as some authors have argued, the companies might earn larger profits in private hands, either as a result of improved efficiency or because the government is willing to decontrol the prices and rates of the goods and services they provide, or because realistic policies are adhered to, which would not happen if they remained under government control. In either case, the fiscal impact of privatization would be positive, provided that taxes are actually paid on the increased profits.

---

[62]The study cited estimates that this change produced an increase of 3.8 percent in receipts in 1988 and 1989. Its effect appears to have been greater in the following years.

On the other hand, privatizing a company that has been steadily losing money (and may continue to do so) could have a positive effect on the subsequent flow of public current revenues. In these circumstances, however, privatization would certainly require that the government incur some prior expenses (capitalization, assumption of some of the debt, compensation to separated personnel, restructuring investments), so that the effect on government cash flow would be the reverse of the usual situation, i.e., negative first and positive afterwards.

Finally, privatization theoretically frees the government from the necessity of making investments in the area in question. This has perhaps been the most frequently used fiscal argument in favor of privatizing public utility companies.[63] It is not always clear, however, what price the state and the community pay to guarantee private investors the conditions necessary to attract investment in these areas (in terms of higher rates or subsidies in the sale of the enterprises), nor what future risks regarding coverage and quality are associated with privatization (which was usually the reason for nationalizing private utility companies in Latin America in the first place).

The inherent difficulty of estimating the above effects is obvious, especially since, with the exception of Chile, privatization is a very recent phenomenon, and also because precise information is difficult to obtain and would require comparison with a non-observable situation (what would have happened had the enterprise remained under government control). The available calculations are based on assumptions and estimates closely reflecting the authors' political viewpoints.

In these conditions, it is difficult to do much more than to present a few general figures and to make a few comments.

Some Practical Data: The Experiences of Chile and Argentina

In Chile in 1974, 257 companies and 3,700 farms that had been nationalized under the Unidad Popular government were returned to the private sector. The fiscal impact of reprivatization was clearly positive since most of the companies and farms were losing money when they were transferred to the public sector and while under its control, and it would have taken time to change this situation. Moreover, the activities in question were of a typically private nature, many were small or medium-sized and it is logical to assume that state management would have been less efficient, from an economic and social point of view, even in the long term.

In the 1975-79 period, another 110 companies in which the government was

---

[63]Of course, there are nonfinancial arguments related to improvements in the quality of the service and fewer opportunities for corruption and favoritism.

the largest shareholder were privatized, most of them banks and commercial and industrial enterprises. The proceeds of the sales totaled approximately $663 million. It is estimated that the government granted a subsidy of about 30 percent on these sales (Foxley, 1983), so that it is unclear whether their fiscal impact in current value was positive.

Between 1985 and 1986, 25 large companies that had been taken over by the government during the financial crisis of 1982 were privatized. The revenue from these sales totaled $1.1 billion, including a subsidy of more than 50 percent (Marcel, 1989). In this case, it is even less clear what the sign of the net fiscal impact was.

In 1986 the fourth stage of the privatization process began with the sale of CORFO shares. This was the most important stage in terms of the amounts involved (close to $1.5 billion up to 1990) and because these companies were traditional public enterprises, most of which generated large surpluses and transferred profits that bolstered public finances.

Some preliminary calculations of the impact of this stage of privatization reveal a negative adjusted net flow for the public sector after 11 years and the existence of a more than 50 percent subsidy in the sale (Marcel, 1989). According to IMF figures, proceeds from the sale of public enterprises represented 3 percent of GDP each year from 1986 to 1989 and 1 percent in 1990[64] (which amounts, recorded as capital earnings instead of deficit financing resources, cause overestimation of the fiscal improvement at the close of the decade and underestimation of the erosion of public revenues in the period); and the direct loss of public current revenues was equivalent to 2.5 percent of GDP per year (operating surplus before deducting the 3 percent taxes less the 0.5 percent taxes) (IMF, 1990). This loss of current revenues will be offset in part by the transfer of public investment outlays to the private sector and by additional taxes if the profits of these enterprises improve under private management.[65]

The conclusions suggested by the above figures are not entirely unexpected since the privatization process in Chile was initiated not with a view to improving public finances but rather to increasing private sector participation, for both economic and political reasons.

This is even more apparent with respect to the fiscal impact of the social insurance reform early in the decade. The reform generated a sizable public cash

---

[64] According to Marcel (1989), total sales between 1986 and 1988 represented 1.87 percent of GDP as an annual average.

[65] Another a priori IMF calculation estimated that the privatization carried out in 1987 would have a negative fiscal impact of 1.6 percent of GDP, offset by a 0.4 percent increase in private sector taxes, a 0.3 percent decrease in transfers to the private sector, dividends from the private sector totaling 0.1 percent, and a 0.7 percent cutback in investments. This would represent a small net loss of 0.1 percent of GDP. These calculations may overestimate the taxes to be paid by the private sector.

deficit as the change was made from a pay-as-you-go to a capitalization system (which required paying or recognizing the liabilities assumed, without the possibility of using new pension contributions to do so) and because the State absorbs the cost of welfare pensions and guarantees contributors a minimum return.[66] Ortuzar (1986) estimated the public deficit generated by the social insurance reform (total of the public sector operating deficit—receipts less pension payments—and the outlays for recognition bonds and welfare pensions) at amounts ranging from 4.5 to 5 percent of GDP in the 1983-97 period and then decreasing gradually. In fact, the deficit of the public social insurance system represented 1.6 percent of GDP in 1979-80 and rose to 6.1 percent of GDP on average between 1981 and 1985. Nevertheless, as the analysis in the section entitled "Adjustment, Investment and Growth" shows, private resources partially financed this deficit (which, however, contributed to the rapid growth of the public debt) and the change in the system sparked a net increase in domestic saving.

Argentina has undertaken a more ambitious privatization program than any other Latin American country.[67] When the program ends in 1994, the government will own only a part of the current state-controlled oil company, the Yacyretá bi-national project currently under construction, the entities of the Atomic Energy Commission and minority shares in other companies.

Lease payments and revenues from the sale of public enterprises totaled $2.194 billion in 1991 and are estimated to reach $5.618 billion in 1992 and 1993 (World Bank, 1992b). These revenues, according to agreements with the IMF, will serve as a kind of bridge financing while a primary structural surplus is accumulated to cover interest payments not financed externally.

The program will involve some initial costs due to the necessity of compensating employees and assuming part of the debts and other liabilities of the enterprises to facilitate their sale. Nevertheless, since most of the privatized

---

[66] The reform lowered the number of contributors in the state system from 2,200,000 to 500,000 between 1980 and 1985, eliminated employer contributions and limited worker contributions to 17 percent of their wages plus a 10 percent voluntary investment to obtain additional benefits. Consequently, the contributions received by the government decreased from 5.6 percent of GDP in 1980 to 2.3 percent in 1985 and 1.7 percent in 1988. At the same time, its outlays increased in some years or decreased only slightly since the new individual capitalization system could not finance the old system's liabilities and the government had to pay "recognition bonds" to compensate contributors who switched to the private system, as well as guaranteeing minimum pensions for those who, with 20 years of service, had not accumulated sufficient savings to cover them ("welfare" pensions) and a minimum level of profitability for private funds (when the latter fail to achieve said minimum profitability they must close, but the difference is made up to contributors by the government).

[67] As of June 1992, two television stations, Aerolíneas Argentinas and the telephone company had been privatized. In addition, YPF's producing oil fields were granted in concession through public bidding. The current program includes the total or partial privatization of the state-controlled metallurgical and petrochemical enterprises, other defense industries, Gas del Estado, electric companies, railroads, the merchant marine, refineries and oil pipelines, etc.

companies had operating deficits (in contrast to the situation in Chile in 1984), the World Bank estimates—perhaps a bit optimistically[68]—that a shift from consolidated deficits of 3.8 percent of GDP in 1989 and 0.4 percent of GDP in 1991 to a surplus of 0.06 percent of GDP will occur in 1994.

Neither the ultimate success of the program nor its net fiscal consequences are yet clear, partly because the authorities were faced with a dilemma: they had initially guaranteed that rates and prices would either be held steady or increased in real terms, which was considered essential for the success of the privatization program, but they subsequently launched a stabilization program legally prohibiting the indexation of contracts, which, to be successful, requires that the nominal growth of prices and public rates remain at a low level (see the section in Chapter Two entitled "Indexation and Inflationary Inertia ").

---

[68] In particular, the World Bank estimates that the privatized enterprises will pay the VAT, income tax and other taxes in amounts equivalent to 0.06 percent of GDP in 1992 and a little more than 0.4 percent of GDP in 1993 and 1994. It does not analyze whether the investment in these enterprises is "additional" or would have generated taxes in other activities.

CHAPTER FIVE

TAX REFORM AND
STRUCTURAL REFORM

Trends in Tax Reform

Reduction and Simplification of Direct Taxes

A review of the tax reform process in Chile, Colombia, Mexico and Argentina suggests several principal trends in direct taxes (Table 5.1):

• Reduction of the rates and simplification of the personal income tax system.
• Reduced rates and the criterion of neutrality in the treatment of capital earnings through the integration of taxes on companies and partners, standardization of the systems for various types of companies, elimination of preferential treatment, and the introduction of adjustments for inflation in company balance sheets and in the financial income and expenditures of individuals.
• Simultaneously, and somewhat contradictorily to the above, the increased use of presumptive systems for taxes on capital earnings, based on the net or gross value of assets.
• The generalization and increased use of withholdings, current or advance payment systems and adjustments for inflation in tax credits and debits in order to moderate the Olivera-Tanzi effect, regularize the flow of tax receipts and

more effectively control evasion. This applies to all taxes but is especially important with respect to direct taxes.
• Generally, receipts of direct taxes tended to decline in the 1980s, but a different trend was noted in some cases in the late 1980s and early 1990s.

Rates, Integration of Business/Partner Taxes and Receipts. The four countries in the sample lowered income tax rates in the 1980s and eliminated the "double taxation" of income by establishing various systems to integrate the taxation of companies and their partners.

In 1984 Chile reduced the maximum rates applicable to individuals and companies to 50 percent and 10 percent, respectively, although the business rate was raised to 15 percent in 1990 (temporarily, until 1994). Companies pay taxes on all profits, while individuals pay taxes on distributed profits and receive a credit for taxes paid within the company. The system and the rate of taxation were different for corporations and limited liability companies. The corporate rate climbed from 30 percent on retained earnings and 20 percent on distributed profits in the 1960s to 35 percent in the early 1970s and 50 percent in 1975, with a 40 percent credit on the tax on dividends paid to individuals.

In 1986 Colombia lowered the maximum rates applicable to individuals and companies to a single, uniform rate of 30 percent, exempting the dividends and profits distributed to individuals. In 1990, however, temporary tax surcharges were levied, which were raised to 25 percent in 1992 (deductible the following year), so that the rate for companies and the highest rate for individuals is currently about 35 percent. The maximum rate for individuals was 52 percent in the 1960s; in 1975 it was raised to 56 percent and in 1983 lowered to 49 percent. Business rates varied according to the type of company and the level of earnings (from a minimum of 20 percent to a maximum of 72 percent, including the excess profits tax) until 1974, when the system was simplified and the rates were fixed at 40 percent for corporations and 20 percent for limited liability companies. The latter was reduced to 18 percent in 1983. Individuals were also required to pay taxes on the profits (distributed and retained) of limited liability companies and on the dividends paid by corporations, although low-income taxpayers were granted a partial discount on the latter.

In 1987 Mexico lowered the top individual rate to 35 percent (from 50 percent and 55 percent in 1986). The business rate (42 percent up to 1987) was lowered to 37 percent in 1989—concurrently with the introduction of balance sheet adjustments for inflation—and then to 36 percent in 1990 and 35 percent in 1991. Starting in 1983 the taxation of companies and of partners was integrated, and while dividends to individuals were still taxable, they could be deducted for corporate income tax purposes. In 1991 the system was changed so that distributed profits and dividends are now tax-exempt for individuals and companies can no longer deduct them.

Argentina reduced the maximum individual rate to 36 percent in 1988 (down from 45 percent) and to 30 percent in 1990, and the business rate from 33 percent to 20 percent, only to raise it again to 30 percent in 1992. Dividends and distributed profits have been tax-exempt for individuals since 1975.

A recent IMF study indicates that the maximum rate for individuals in a sample of 18 Latin American countries was 48 percent as a simple average in 1979 and 35.4 percent in 1991. In 1979 the marginal rate exceeded 40 percent in all the countries and 50 percent in 12; in 1991 there were maximum marginal rates of 25 percent in three countries (Brazil, Costa Rica and Ecuador), 30 percent in three others (Argentina, Colombia—not counting the surcharge—and Paraguay) and 50 percent or more in only four (Chile, El Salvador, Nicaragua, and Panama).

The simple average for companies fell from 43.5 percent in 1980 to 36.3 percent in 1991. In 1980 the lowest maximum rate for companies was 30 percent or less in three countries (Bolivia, Ecuador and Uruguay); this was the case in seven countries in 1991. It was 40 percent or more in 12 countries in 1981, however, and remains at this level today in only four.

As for taxes on foreign investment, most of the countries still have a capital remittance tax, although the rate decreased as a simple average from 16.6 percent in 1980 to 10.6 percent in 1991 (IMF, 1980-92). In most cases the rate was lowered in such a way that the total tax (regular rate plus the remittance tax applied to distributed profits) does not exceed the U.S. rate.

In Chile, foreign companies can opt for a fixed rate of 49.5 percent or 40 percent plus a variable remittance tax. In Argentina, foreign capital is taxed at 36 percent and there is a 20 percent tax on remittances. In Mexico, dividends to non-residents are taxed at 35 percent. In Colombia, the remittance tax was fixed at 20 percent in 1974, raised to 36 percent in 1986, lowered to 12 percent in 1990, and will be gradually decreased between 1993 and 1997 to 7 percent (except in the petroleum industry, where it will remain at 12 percent).

Income tax receipts (personal and corporate) decreased as a percentage of GDP in 15 of the 18 countries studied by the IMF (exceptions were Colombia, Guatemala, and Jamaica). These receipts are below 1 percent of GDP in Bolivia and Peru and over 5 percent of GDP in Mexico (excluding direct taxes on oil, copper, and other minerals). In Argentina they were 1.3 percent of GDP, in Chile 2.9 percent (excluding copper), and in Colombia 4.5 percent.

These percentages are low on the international scale. For a sample of 86 developing countries, Tanzi (in Bird and Oldman, 1990) calculated an average of 5.6 percent of GDP and, for countries in the same income group as the four included in this sample, 5.75 percent and 8.08 percent of GDP.

Simplification, Adjustments for Inflation, and Presumptive Systems.   Other common characteristics of income tax reform in Latin America are the search for simpler, more easily managed structures, the gradual introduction

Table 5.1 Tax System Trends

	Min. indiv. rate		Level of indiv. exemptions (per capita GDP)		Business rate		Tax on business assets						Remittance of profits tax[3]		VAT or sales tax		
							1980			1990							
	1979	1991	1979	1991[1]	1980	1991	Rate	Addl. Min. or Sub.	Net or gross assets (partial)[3]	Rate	Addl. Min. or Sub.	Net or gross assets (partial)[3]	1980	1990	1980	1990	1992
Argentina	45	30	0.70	4.70	33	20	1.5	A	N	1	M	G	28.5	20	16	18	
Bolivia	48	10	0.12	—	30	[a]	—	—	—	3	S	N	30	—	2.10	10	
Brazil	55	25	0.67	1.16	35	42.95–51.7	—	—	—	—	—	—	25	17; 12,16[e]; 5[f]	8.10[d]; 7,17,20; 5	10–15	
Chile	60	50	0.50	2.26	48–57	15	—	—	—	—	—	—	7.4	—	20	18	
Colombia	56	30	0.36	0.41	40	30	3.2	M	N	7	M	N	20	19	6,15,35[g]	6,10,35	14[f]
Costa Rica	50	25	0.20	2.85	5–45	30	0.3–1.05	A	GP	0.36–1.17	A	GP	15	15	8.0	10	
Dom. Rep.	72	70	—	0.17	20–55	30	—	—	—	—	—	—	21	21	—	6	
Ecuador	50	25	0.24	2.87	15–43	12.3–49.4	0.16	A	G	0.15	A	N	25	—	5	10	
El Salvador	60	50	—	2.34	20	25–36	0.1–1.4	A	N	0.9–2	A	G	10	11.4	5[h]	—[g]	
Guatemala	58	34	—	2.34	15.5–43	10–30	0.3–0.8	A	GP	0.3–0.9	A	GP	15	12.5	2	7	
Honduras	40	40	—	6.87	33.8–52.8	12–34	—	—	—	—	—	—	21	15	—	7–10	
Mexico	55	35	—	0.18	42	37	—	—	—	2	M	G	—	—	10	6,15,20	
Nicaragua	50	60	—	—	5–42	35	1	A	GP	1–3	A	N	—	20	8	10,15,25	
Panama	56	56	0.52	0.49	6–50	40–50	—	—	—	1	A	N	—	—	—	5	

Table 5.1 (cont.)

	DIRECT TAXES														INDIRECT TAXES		
	Min. indiv. rate		Level of indiv. exemptions (per capita GDP)		Business rate		Tax on business assets						Remittance of profits tax		VAT or sales tax		
							1980			1990							
	1979	1991	1979	1991[1]	1980	1991	Rate	Addl. Min. or Sub.	Net or gross assets (partial)[3]	Rate	Addl. Min. or Sub.	Net or gross assets (partial)[3]	1980	1990	1980	1990	1992
Paraguay	Exempt	30	Exempt	—	20-50	20-50	1	A	GP	1[b]	A	GP	10	10	3, 5, 10	—	—
Peru	56	37	0.08	—	25-30	25-35	—	—	—	1.5-3	—	N-B[c]	30	10	6, 22, 42	12	—
Uruguay	Exempt	Exempt	Exempt	Exempt	25	30	4.5	A	N	2	A	N	20	—	8, 18	12, 21	—
Venezuela	45	30	1.09	1.96	18-50	15-50	—	—	—	—	—	—	20	20	—	—	—
Simple Average	48.1	35.4	0.45	1.62	43.5[2]	36.3[2]						16.6	10.6				

[1] Most correspond to 1990 laws, so they apply to 1991 income. Some laws, however, may have been amended since.
[2] In countries with graduated rates, the maximum rate was used to calculate the simple average.
[3] Fixed assets tax in Costa Rica and real property tax in Guatemala, Nicaragua and Paraguay.
[a] Bolivia replaced the tax on companies with a 3 percent net assets tax.
[b] This tax is in the form of a license to do business; the maximum amount is $20,000 per year.
[c] This is a cross between a gross assets tax and a net assets tax since only half of the liabilities can be deducted from the taxable base.
[d] Collected by the central government.
[e] Collected by the State.
[f] Collected by the municipality.
[g] This 15 percent applies to manufacturing, which is the equivalent of a 10 percent consumer tax. The 1992 tax became effective in 1993.
[h] At present, the 5 percent tax on business turnover is still being collected.
Sources: Shome, 1992. Case studies.

Table 5.2. Structure of Tax Receipts
(Percentage of GDP)

	Income		VAT		Specific products		Foreign trade		Others		Social Security		Total central government		Total general government	
	1980	1990	1980	1990	1980	1990	1980	1990	1980	1990	1980	1990	1980	1990	1980	1990
Argentina¹ᵃ	2.4	1.2	4.3	2.8	3.0	1.7	2.1	2.2	1.5	2.7	5.4	4.4	18.7	15.0	23.9	16.6ᵇ
Brazil²	3.0	3.9	n.a.	n.a.	n.a.	n.a.	1.5	0.4	0.8	2.2	6.1	5.0	17.4	8.6	22.0	24.1
Chile	7.3	6.7	10.2	8.9	1.3	2.1	2.0	2.8	0.5	0.7	5.6	1.9	25.3	—	26.4	23.1ᵇ
Costa Rica	2.4	2.3	1.7	3.0	3.8	3.1	3.4	5.3	0.2	—	5.1	6.6	16.8	19.7	17.1	21.1
Jamaica³	10.0	11.5	5.8	n.a.	7.2	n.a.	0.9	5.4	0.7	—	1.0	—	27.0	26.8	n.a.	n.a.
Uruguay³	2.3	1.6	5.7	6.6	3.8	3.0	2.1	0.9	1.0	1.2	5.2	6.5	21.0	21.2	n.a.	n.a.
Colombia	3.0	3.9	1.9	2.8	0.7	0.7	2.5	1.9	0.3	0.2	1.4	1.6	9.8	11.1	12.9	14.2
Dominican Republic⁴	2.8	3.0	0.6	0.7	2.5	2.1	4.4	5.9	0.3	0.6	0.5	0.6	11.1	13.0	11.2	n.a.
Ecuador	5.7	9.3	1.5	2.8	0.7	0.6	3.9	2.3	0.4	0.7	0.0	0.0	12.3	16.0	n.a.	n.a.
Mexico³	5.5	5.5	2.6	3.0	1.2	2.4	1.0	0.8	4.0	5.3ᶜ	2.3	2.2	16.6	19.2	17.2	18.8
Panama³	5.8	3.2	1.9	1.2	2.0	1.8	2.8	1.8	1.0	1.1	5.7	6.0	19.9	15.7	20.3	16.3
Venezuela³	18.0	12.3	—	—	1.0	0.8	1.8	1.6	—	—	1.2	0.6	22.2	15.4	n.a.	n.a.
Bolivia	0.0	0.6	0.0	2.2	1.9	2.2	1.0	0.9	—	—	1.0	1.1	2.9	6.6	4.5	7.9
Guatemala³	1.3	1.7	1.5	1.2	1.2	0.8	3.4	3.2	0.5	0.5	1.3	0.0	10.1	7.8	10.6	n.a.
Nicaragua	1.8	1.5	2.2	0.9	3.6	2.3	5.8	1.5	0.5	0.5	2.0	1.0	20.1	6.1	n.a.	8.1
Paraguay	1.8	1.5	0.6	0.8	1.2	1.9	2.7	2.4	—	—	1.4	1.5	10.1	10.4	10.4	n.a.
Peru	6.0	0.6	5.7	n.a.	1.8	n.a.	5.6	1.5	—	—	2.2	—	18.9	7.9	22.1	n.a.

n.a. not available
¹ The figure for the last year (1990) is actually for 1991.
² The figure for the last year (1990) is actually for 1990-91.
³ The figure for the last year (1990) is actually for 1989.
⁴ The figure for the last year (1990) is actually for 1988.
ᵃExcluding provinces.
ᵇNonfinancial public sector.
ᶜIncludes taxes on petroleum and natural gas production and commercial use.
Source: Shome (1992).

of adjustments for inflation, and the increasing use of presumptive systems.

The objective of structural simplification has been to facilitate administrative control, reduce collection costs and increase the horizontal equity and "neutrality" of the system. In most cases, this has been accomplished in a variety of ways: standardization of taxes, systems and rates; elimination of special exemptions and preferential systems; standardization of personal deductions and exemptions and increasing the minimum exemption level in order to reduce the number of minor contributors handled by the administration, which is then able to concentrate on auditing major contributors.

Thus, for example, in the countries studied by the IMF, the minimum exemption level was raised substantially: from an average of 0.45 percent of per capita income in 1979 to 1.72 percent in 1991.

There were various reasons for and stages in the introduction of adjustments for inflation. The pioneers in this field were the countries that had experienced high levels of inflation: Argentina, Brazil and, most especially, Chile.

In the early stages, typically, tax brackets and deductions or exemptions with a fixed value or ceiling were indexed to preserve the original proportionality and progressivity, thus avoiding the inflationary effect that would have led to an inordinate increase in the number of contributors and placed too many of them in the highest marginal tax brackets. This effect (inflation creep) encouraged evasion (Perry and Cárdenas, 1986) and led to frequent changes in the amounts and characteristics of the deductions and exemptions, making the system increasingly difficulty to manage and creating greater horizontal inequities. These adjustments therefore helped simplify and stabilize the legal structure of the tax. The four countries in the sample incorporated adjustments of this type in their legislation around 1980.

Tax credits and debits were generally indexed simultaneously to moderate the Olivera-Tanzi effect. The generalized use and expanded coverage of withholdings and current and advance payment systems had the same purpose. Again, the four countries in the sample incorporated adjustments of this type in their legislation in the early 1980s. In some countries both types of adjustments were effected by determining and recording the amount of taxable income, deductions and taxes in "tax units," indexed on the basis of inflation.

Adjustments for inflation in the cost (or value) of fixed assets for the purpose of computing capital gains (in countries that had capital gains taxes), deductions for depreciation, and real estate and net worth taxes also made an early appearance. Some countries, however, chose other, partial solutions such as accelerated depreciation and LIFO inventory systems.

More recent is the widespread practice of allowing companies to adjust their financial flows for inflation and to make across-the-board adjustments for inflation in their balance sheets. This practice is a result of the mounting evidence concerning the effects of the tax system on the financial structure of companies, which, by allowing the deduction of nominal interest, encouraged companies to incur excessive debt, increasing their vulnerability in times of crisis, creating an excessive demand for credit (which complicated macroeconomic management) and rendering the growth of the financial market uncertain. The higher and more variable the rate of inflation, the more pronounced these effects were (Boskin and McLure, 1990). Moreover, financial deregulation and the greater mobility of capital made it necessary to adjust the taxes on interest earned to keep them internationally competitive.

In 1975 Chile adopted a comprehensive system of adjustments for inflation in company balance sheets, which was a coherent, simple and elegant solution to most of these problems. Prior to that time, several countries had adopted partial solutions that perpetuated certain biases and introduced some new ones. The Chilean model was the prototype of the comprehensive adjustment systems recently established by countries such as Mexico (1987 to 1989), Ecuador (1991) and Colombia (1992).

The recent trend toward establishing general systems based on a presumptive minimum income or tax originated with the 1974 tax reform in Colombia. In light of the unsuccessful experiment with partial presumptive systems based on the value of land in the agricultural and livestock sector, the focus was shifted to the presumption of a minimum return on the net worth of any taxpayer (initially 8 percent, then lowered to 4 percent with the indexation of company balance sheets), which could be waived only in cases of force majeure, long-term investments, or if government controls and prohibitions prevented obtaining the predetermined minimum return. The Colombian system permits deferring declared losses for up to five years, provided that the taxable income does not fall below the presumptive minimum in any of the five years.

The Colombian experiment was very successful, although there were some problems with verifying declared liabilities (Perry and Cárdenas, 1986). This same experiment was subsequently used in the Bolivian tax reform of 1985, in which the business income tax (given its minimal yield) was completely replaced with a presumptive system. The presumptive tax was set at 3 percent of net worth. The lack of net worth declarations by individuals precluded application of the presumptive system to them, as was done in Colombia.

Finally, the IMF recognized the Colombian and Bolivian experiments and has been recommending the adoption of similar systems, although, for reasons of administrative control, among others (see below), it has promoted establishment of presumptive systems based not on net assets but on gross assets. Mexico in 1990 and Argentina in 1991 adopted this system, with rates of 2 percent in the former instance and 1 percent in the latter. In both cases, the system was limited to companies, as it was in Bolivia, since there was as yet no system for the declaration of net worth by individuals.

Property and Net Worth Taxes.   Property taxes have not figured significantly in the tax structure of Latin American countries (for an overview of the structure of tax receipts, see Table 5.2). In all other respects, the recent trend in the region is unclear. Although some countries eliminated taxes on net or gross assets, they still exist in others (in eight of the 18 countries studied by the IMF) and the trend toward establishing a minimum income tax system based on net or gross assets can be interpreted as an approximate form of property taxation. The four countries of the sample abolished the tax on net worth (which was highly productive in Colombia, where it applied only to individuals),[69] but three of them now have a system based on a presumed return on net or gross assets.

Likewise, the trend toward greater fiscal decentralization has rekindled interest in boosting real estate taxes at the municipal level. Some countries have introduced systems for the indexation of assessments or self-assessments to shield receipts of these taxes—formerly based on administrative cadastral assessments made at intervals greater than five years—from the effects of inflation.

Generalization and Expanded Coverage of the VAT

In the last 20 years, most Latin American countries replaced their sales or turnover taxes, whether single-stage or cumulative, characterized by a multiplicity of rates and systems, with a value added tax (VAT) with a much smaller number of categories and rates. Three of the countries in the sample did so in the mid-1970s (Colombia in 1974, Argentina and Chile in 1975), followed by Mexico in 1980. A recent IMF study on tax policy trends in Latin America in the last decade (Shome, 1992) shows that in 1980, of 18 countries, eight had some form of VAT based on the credit principle. In 1991 the number had grown to 15, and two others had bills in the approval process (El Salvador and Venezuela). In most countries the change led to a net increase in receipts.

Generally, at the outset, a "credit type" VAT was adopted (which allows crediting the taxes paid on the purchase of inputs against the amount paid on taxable sales) as well as a "consumption type" VAT (which allows immediate credit for taxes paid on the purchase of capital goods) and tax refunds for products taxed at a zero rate, exports in particular. The countries that started out with several variants of these measures (such as Colombia) changed the structure of the tax to fit this model.

Once the VAT was established, its coverage was gradually expanded by various methods:

• Generally, the lists of excluded or exempted goods —and services— were shortened (although the opposite sometimes occurred, as in Argentina with its Industrial Promotion Law).

---

[69] This was the most widely debated tax reform in recent years in Colombia. See, for example, Boskin and McLure (1990).

• Various countries replaced the initial exemptions for small companies or businesses with simplified systems, focused more on improving overall control of the tax than on taxing added value in these establishments.
• Some countries in which the VAT was initially applied to a short list of services lengthened the list as time went on—including, for example, public, financial and transportation services and certain personal services—or subsequently reduced the number of exemptions.
• Some countries that started out with a VAT in the manufacturing sector later extended it to retail trade (as was the case, once again, in Colombia).

The general rate of the VAT and its share in national tax receipts varied greatly from one country to another and from one period to another. In many countries, both have increased constantly. Among the countries in the sample, this was the case in Colombia, where the basic rate went from 10 percent in 1983 —and the earlier 15 percent in the manufacturing sector— to 12 percent in 1990 and will be 14 percent in 1993, and where VAT receipts increased 0.7 percent of GDP in the 1980s and continued expanding in 1991 and 1992. In other countries there were periods of ups and downs. In Mexico, the basic rate went from 10 percent in 1980 to 15 percent in 1983 and fell back to 10 percent in 1992. Receipts decreased from 1980 to 1982, regained their 1980 level between 1983 and 1987, and then increased, especially in 1990. In Chile, the basic rate fell from 20 percent (1975) to 16 percent in 1988 and then climbed to 18 percent in 1990, while receipts dropped 2 percent of GDP in the 1980s and then recovered somewhat in 1991. In Argentina the basic rate rose from 13 percent in 1975 to 20 percent in 1980, fell to 15 percent in 1988 and 13 percent in 1990, and then rose again to 16 percent in 1991 and 18 percent in 1992. Receipts varied widely during the decade, with an overall downward trend (in 1989 they were 3.4 percent of GDP less than in 1981), but rallied significantly in 1991 (nearly reaching their 1981 level).

In the above-cited IMF study, it was found that of the eight countries with a value added tax in 1980, the basic rate was higher in 1991 than in 1980 in six of them and lower in two. The basic rates varied widely: from 5 to 7 percent (Dominican Republic, Guatemala, and Panama) to 18 percent (Argentina and Chile).

As far as the rate structure is concerned, nine of the 15 countries with value added taxes in 1991 had uniform rates. In the others, foods and essential consumer goods were typically exempted or had a zero or reduced rate, while the highest rates (20 to 35 percent) were applied to "luxury" goods (automobiles, yachts, jewelry) or products such as alcoholic beverages.

Receipts (of VAT or sales tax) increased as a percentage of GDP in nine countries and decreased in six, ranging at the end of the decade from 0.7 percent to 9 percent of GDP (Dominican Republic and Chile, respectively), with the majority situated between 1 percent of GDP and 5 percent of GDP (in the sample: Argentina, 5 percent in 1991; Mexico, 3.5 percent; and Colombia, 3.1 percent). The size of the VAT in the large countries of the region is thus greater than the average for the 86 developing countries in Tanzi's sample (2.1 percent of GDP) and even the highest income group (3.1 percent of GDP), in contrast to the experience with direct taxes. VAT receipts in Chile are even similar to the receipts in industrialized countries and are much more productive than those of the other countries of the region, in proportion to the basic rate. These facts reveal the high degree of coverage and compliance Chile has achieved in the administration of this tax. Mexico and Argentina have made considerable strides very recently in terms of the administration and productivity of the tax, but they are still far below the Chilean levels.

The Reform of Other Indirect Taxes

In addition to the generalization of the VAT and the expansion of its coverage, other trends in indirect taxation have been observed:

• The lowering of tariffs and the elimination of other import and export taxes as part of the trade liberalization process analyzed in Chapter Three.
• The reinforcement and modernization of certain excise taxes (fuel taxes in particular).
• The reduction or elimination of a large number of minor taxes.

Thus, most indirect taxation has focused on the VAT and a few excise taxes (fuel, alcohol, beer, soft drinks, tobacco, automobiles), which are convenient fiscal tools (easy to administer and fiscally productive) that can be justified in terms of economic efficiency: compensation for negative externalities (alcoholic beverages, tobacco, environmental costs) and as user taxes (fuels and automobiles).

The increasing taxation of fuels warrants special comment. Generally, fuel taxes are high in countries that are not net exporters of petroleum and petroleum by-products (Argentina, Brazil, Chile, and Uruguay) and low in exporting countries (Colombia, Ecuador, Venezuela, and until recently, Mexico and Peru). The sizes of the government and the price control, however, are such that in various countries the real tax paid by consumers is much lower than the rate would suggest, and is even negative in certain periods.

In fact, the price to the consumer has often been lower than the opportunity cost of fuels —import CIF or export FOB, plus shipping and distribution costs—so that all or most of the "tax" is paid by the state oil company (this was the case in Argentina, Colombia, Ecuador, and Peru). Thus, it has been more a question of an intergovernmental transfer than an excise tax. When the state oil company failed to generate sufficient surpluses, these taxes led to its financial collapse and the contraction of investment in the sector (as was the case in Ecuador, Peru and Argentina), or else other transfers or "payments" from the state were required (such was the case in Colombia between 1975 and 1985, when the country was a net importer, and in Argentina, where in some years government payments to YPF were larger than the total tax collected).

In recent years there has been a trend toward decontrolling prices or conforming them to international prices, so that fuel taxes are beginning to behave like true excise taxes. In some of the exporting countries (Colombia, Ecuador, and Venezuela), however, prices still lag behind.

Chronology of the Reforms

The tax reform process in Latin America occurred in waves. Various countries launched ambitious tax reforms in the mid-1970s when the pursuit of expansive fiscal policies had created substantial deficits and inflation was spiraling upward, partly because of these policies and partly because of the acceleration of international inflation. This was the case in three of the four countries in the sample: Colombia in 1974 and Argentina and Chile in 1975. It was at that time that the VAT was introduced in these three countries,[70] adjustments for inflation were adopted in Argentina and Chile and on the horizon in Colombia,[71] and the first steps were taken toward greater neutrality in taxation through standardization, simplification of rate structures, deductions and exemptions,[72] and toward the generalization of withholdings and current and advance payment systems. Colombia introduced its first presumptive minimum income system based on the net worth of companies and individuals.

In Mexico, the same process occurred between 1978 and 1981: the VAT was introduced in 1980 and similar steps were taken with respect to direct taxes.

A second wave occurred in the mid-1980s. Chile in 1984 and Bolivia in 1985 were the first to lower the rates of their direct taxes and to reduce the tax on capital earnings; Colombia followed suit in 1986, as did Mexico in 1987. Bolivia introduced the VAT at this time as well as a tax on assets. Mexico adopted a system of adjustments for inflation similar to the one in Chile, and Colombia expanded its system to include the treatment of financial flows (and then, in 1992, adopted a comprehensive system similar to Chile's). In Ar-

---

[70] Although in Colombia it was limited to the manufacturing sector until 1983.

[71] In Colombia, the costs of assets were indexed for purposes of the capital gains tax, as were tax credits and debits and the structure of rates and deductions. In Argentina, depreciation, losses and the treatment of financial income and expenditures were also indexed. Chile adopted a comprehensive system of adjustments for inflation in company balance sheets, which, because of their simplicity and elegance, were later imitated in other Latin American countries.

[72] Although their number increased again in Colombia and, more especially, in Argentina.

gentina, bills were drafted on this subject between 1985 and 1987, although none of them were successful.

A third wave of reforms began in 1990, aimed at increasing VAT and income tax receipts in the four countries in the sample and in several others in the region, as well as generalization of the presumptive tax on assets.

Issues and Objectives

Reasons for the Recent Trends: Adaptation of the Tax System to the Requirements of Structural Reform

There were various reasons for the aforementioned trends. The objective of administrative simplicity (to curb evasion, reduce the costs of collection and limit opportunities for corruption) and the need for receipts following the fiscal crisis in the 1980s were perhaps the most compelling. Another factor was the criterion of neutrality in government action, in contrast to the more interventionist role characteristic of economic thinking in Latin America in earlier decades. The focus of "supply-side economics" was on the reduction of direct taxes and lower capital earnings taxes. Nevertheless, adaptation of the tax system to the requirements of structural reform played an increasingly significant role.

This is particularly true with respect to trade liberalization and financial deregulation. As explained in Chapter Three, trade reform led to the gradual abandonment of taxes on foreign trade (although, in some cases, receipts of such taxes increased temporarily) and their replacement by domestic taxes, particularly the VAT. Moreover, one of the key objectives of trade liberalization, i.e. the elimination of the existing biases against exports, reinforced the trend toward the adoption of a credit type VAT and the refund of taxes paid on inputs used in exports, which is the only effective way (along with drawback systems) of avoiding the effect of indirect taxes on the costs of exportable output.

Liberalization also had a significant impact on the orientation of changes in direct taxation. The reduction of the rates of direct taxes was partly a concession to administrative realities and partly influenced by the belief that direct taxes (or, more precisely, positive marginal rates) discouraged productive effort. Nevertheless, it was given a final push by the 1986 tax reform in the United States.

More and more Latin American countries attempted to adapt the levels and structure of their direct taxes to those of their principal trading partner and the source of most of the flows of direct foreign investment in the region. This consideration has been particularly important with respect to the reform of taxes on capital earnings, the objective of which is to eliminate biases against the free movement of financial and investment flows and to attract such flows. It was initially thought that the U.S. reform would have a similar effect on its European and Asian partners and competitors, but such was not the case. It is not entirely clear, therefore, why the Latin American countries felt the need to conform their tax systems to the U.S. standard, unless it was because the prospects of hemispheric economic integration were rapidly coming into focus.

In the long term, the objectives of the structural reform process, particularly trade liberalization and financial deregulation, made it necessary to increase the receipts of basic taxes (income and VAT), as a result of:

- The growing conviction that a permanent and credible fiscal adjustment was necessary for the equilibrium of an open economy.
- The need to increase or sustain investment in physical infrastructure and human capital in order to improve the international competitiveness of the productive sector, which precluded fiscal adjustments based on additional cuts in public spending and, consequently, necessitated raising the level of tax receipts.
- The temporary nature of the inflow of capital from privatization and the use and abuse of minor taxes that have adverse effects on economic efficiency.
- The possible need to replace taxes on foreign trade with domestic taxes and to avoid taxes on exchange and financial transactions, given the objectives of trade liberalization and financial deregulation.
- The need to generate fiscal surpluses to accommodate the heavy inflow of capital since 1991.

Moreover, trade liberalization and financial deregulation have prompted efforts to boost income tax and VAT receipts, in particular through improvements in administration, increases in coverage, the reduction of exemptions and other concessions, the generalization of withholding systems and the use of presumptive systems, for only in this way can the dilemma of avoiding very high marginal rates while at the same time obtaining the fiscal resources necessary for the above purposes be resolved. The recent trend toward stepping up administrative efforts in Argentina and Mexico is enlightening in this regard.

Topics Related to Economic Efficiency

The general direction of the above-mentioned trends has been toward reducing the efficiency costs inherent in any tax system. Nevertheless, there are still some significant concerns in this regard. In particular, the fact that in most cases the VAT legally excludes the primary sectors and (in fact or by law) the informal sectors of industry and commerce can create serious distortions and inefficiency in the allocation of resources. These effects have not been sufficiently studied and are not taken into account when a value added tax is recommended and adopted as the centerpiece of the tax system.

The same is true of the growing tendency to recommend and establish minimum tax systems based on gross assets. This practice, in contrast to the presumptive minimum tax based on net worth originally adopted in Bolivia and Colombia, can create a substantial bias against new companies, which are far more likely than established companies to finance their investment with loans, whereas the latter can rely in part on retained earnings.

The presumptive tax on net assets has a clear, theoretical justification, as indicated in several studies (Sadka and Tanzi, 1992; Perry and Cárdenas, 1986). In fact, the market, when resources are being allocated efficiently, tends to level the internal rate of return on marginal investments in economic activities having the same degree of risk, so that the minimum presumptive tax on net assets theoretically places an effective constraint on evasion. Moreover, if there are assets with yields below a reasonable minimum, the tax becomes an incentive to improve their yield and the economic efficiency of investments. This type of incentive would be even greater if the presumptive tax entirely replaced the income tax (as in Bolivia), but in this case other advantages of the tax (in terms of receipts and equity) would be lost.

There are no solid theoretical arguments to justify basing this type of tax on gross assets.[73] It is argued that this would constitute an incentive for the increased capitalization of companies; however, it is one thing to eliminate biases against capitalization in favor of indebtedness, as in the case of the full deduction of nominal interest in inflationary periods,[74] and another thing altogether to introduce artificial biases against indebtedness in favor of capitalization. Such a distortion exposes investors to greater risks and drives up the cost of investment, which can ultimately affect both its composition and its level.

Distribution

The growing disillusionment in the 1970s and early 1980s with the presumed distributive effects of the graduated rate structure of income tax and even of indirect taxes contributed to the ascendancy of the objectives of simplification and collection and, consequently, the above-mentioned reforms. Today, the opposite view seems to be gaining ground: the new tax structure may have ex-

---

[73] As its advocates acknowledge when they claim that "from the administrative viewpoint, it is maintained that the tax should focus on measurable assets and should involve gross rather than net assets" (Sadka and Tanzi, 1992).

[74] The solution in this case, of course, is to introduce appropriate adjustments for inflation and not to try to compensate for one imperfection with another, as the above-cited IMF study proposes.

cessively and unnecessarily downplayed the importance of the distributive criteria.[75]

The fact that, in recent years, at least two of the four countries in the sample (Chile and Colombia) raised the rates of direct taxes and all four have actively looked for ways to increase their receipts, partially reversing the trends of the previous decade, suggests that one of the objectives of tax policy may be a more balanced approach.

In the mid-1980s, after the Chilean and Bolivian reforms of 1984 and 1985, respectively, it was widely believed that tax systems in Latin America would focus exclusively on taxing consumption and indirect taxes and that income taxes would be gradually phased out. Few people think that way today, although there is some speculation about a possible shift to the taxation of cash flows, which would eliminate the capital earnings tax entirely.[76]

New Issues

Two other issues, in addition to the above, are foreseeable and will dominate the discussion of taxes in Latin American countries in the next decade. The first is the topic of tax coordination and harmonization between countries as part of economic integration plans. The members of the European Community found it necessary to move in this direction years ago: the agreement on the generalized adoption of a consumer and credit type VAT with a minimum rate has to date been the most well-known decision made by the Community on this subject; nevertheless, agreements on subsidies and economic competition have ruled out tax and fiscal concessions as a means of attracting investment at the expense of other countries. Today, the possible harmonization of fuel taxes is also being discussed as a way of avoiding distortions in transport costs and for environmental reasons. Some Latin American countries are beginning to experience problems because of the dissimilarity of tax systems and government subsidies between countries that have concluded integration agreements, as is the case, for example, between Colombia and Venezuela and between Argentina and Brazil.

Another topic that will be gaining importance is that of pollution "taxes" or "rates" (or similar systems such as negotiable emissions permits), possibly in the industrialized countries first —where they are already a topic of public debate —and then in the developing countries. Environmental taxes have the

---

[75] The relative abandonment of distributive objectives was also related to the obvious difficulty of determining the actual impact of the taxes using the partial equilibrium methods of analysis prevalent until the early 1980s; recent interest was generated by the greater reliability of the estimates provided by computable general equilibrium models.

[76] This proposal by McLure, among others, has been gaining acceptance in institutions such as the IMF. See Shome (1992).

enormous theoretical advantage not only of not causing losses in economic efficiency, as is true of almost every other kind of tax, but, quite the contrary, of facilitating efficiency gains insofar as they closely approximate the costs of the negative externalities of pollution and the deterioration of natural resources. The major obstacle to the development of these taxes will be the requirement of a minimum level of international coordination since countries that do not levy them will be artificially increasing their competitiveness through a subsidy equivalent to the environmental cost not collected from polluters. In other words, this will become a critical topic in the field of trade relations and, therefore, an additional link between the processes of trade liberalization and public finances.

CHAPTER SIX

CONCLUSIONS

Disequilibrium and Subsequent Fiscal Adjustment in the 1980s

External variables had a considerable, direct impact, both in the processes of disequilibrium and in the subsequent adjustment. This was particularly true of the deterioration in the early 1980s in the terms of trade and the subsequent improvement in countries whose public finances relied heavily on revenue from their main export product (such as Chile, Colombia, and Mexico).

Furthermore, rising international interest rates and the ensuing suspension of flows from commercial banks placed severe restrictions on public finances, especially in countries that had previously incurred large external debts.

The economic crisis experienced by most of the countries as a result of the overlapping of these external shocks with growing macroeconomic disequilibria and the adjustment programs themselves also had a substantial impact on the trend of public finances. In particular, the acceleration of inflationary processes, recession, the contraction of imports, capital flight and, in some countries, demonetization, had a pronounced effect on revenue. Moreover, the financial crisis and the hike in domestic interest rates generated sizable quasi-fiscal deficits (except in Colombia) and considerable increases in the service of domestic debt (especially in Argentina and Mexico) and in subsidies to the private sector (especially in Argentina and Chile).

On the other hand, the ultimate success of stabilization programs and the start of economic recovery in some countries contributed significantly to the subsequent fiscal adjustment.

Exchange management played a very important role with respect to fiscal equilibrium. In countries where the public sector is a net exporter of goods and services (such as Chile, Mexico and Colombia), the real devaluation required for the adjustment of the external sector contributed enormously to the fiscal adjustment. The opposite occurred in Argentina. This fact appears to have been a major determinant of the differences in exchange management in the countries studied, particularly at the end of the decade.

The inability of autonomous fiscal policy to react in a timely manner to the disequilibria caused by internal and external shocks (due to the lag between the making of a decision and its effects) and, in some cases, the expansive fiscal policy of the early 1980s, intensified the erosion of public finances or slowed their adjustment.

The countries reacted to fiscal deficits primarily by cutting expenses (except Colombia) and, initially, by raising public sector prices and rates and taxes other than income tax and the VAT (on foreign trade, energy products and exchange and financial transactions). It was only in the late 1980s or early 1990s that all the countries started raising basic taxes again (income tax and VAT), prompted by the growing conviction that a permanent and credible fiscal adjustment was essential to the equilibrium of an open economy.

Fiscal Adjustment, Stabilization, and Exchange and Fiscal Dilemmas in Open Economies

Experience demonstrates the fundamental importance of fiscal adjustment in stabilization programs, but it also shows that the relationship between fiscal equilibrium or adjustment and stabilization has not always been a close one. There are three reasons for this, each of which has important implications for the management of public finances:

• Since their public finances depend on the revenue from major commodities exports, the fiscal balance of various countries tends to behave anti-cyclically. If the autonomous fiscal policy is not neutral with respect to these variations, public finances deteriorate as economic activity contracts and inflation falls;

conversely, the fiscal accounts improve as demand heats up, stimulating economic recovery and fueling inflation.

This fact points to the necessity of finding a way of automatically stabilizing public spending and the real exchange rate, despite fluctuations in the price of major commodities exports. Furthermore, the goals of stabilization programs must take these cyclical characteristics into account, in order to prevent public finances from behaving pro-cyclically. Neither the governments of Latin America nor the multilateral institutions have given sufficient thought to this problem.

• Inflationary inertia—caused by the shortening of contractual periods and the routine use of indexation clauses and procedures based on the prior period's inflation—undermined conventional stabilization programs (based exclusively on fiscal and monetary adjustment) and intensified the inflationary effect of variations in the real exchange rate (and in relative prices in general). Consequently, countries with soaring inflation rates and a high degree of indexation were forced to adopt unorthodox stabilization programs combining fiscal and monetary adjustment with a fixed exchange rate and wage and price policies.
• This was not enough, however, in countries that had accumulated a sizable public debt as a result of persistent fiscal and quasifiscal deficits (Argentina and Mexico). In these cases, expectations of a possible devaluation and the repudiation of the public debt, whether explicit or implicit (as in the case of domestic debt, through the acceleration of inflation), stalled unconventional stabilization programs until steps were taken to lighten the burden of domestic[77] and external[78] debt.

Two difficulties were encountered in implementing unconventional stabilization programs:

• Exchange appreciation, caused by the slow convergence of domestic and international inflation rates, can sometimes provoke an exchange crisis, as it did in Argentina in 1981 and 1988 and in Chile in 1981.

In the present circumstances, this possibility depends on (i) how fast inflation rates converge, (ii) whether the capital inflow is temporary or permanent, and (iii) whether it is financing increases in investment or increases in consumption.

---

[77] This was accomplished through the change of the due dates of domestic debt in Mexico and the mandatory conversion of domestic debt instruments into BONEXes in Argentina.
[78] This was accomplished through the Brady Plan, especially in Mexico.

• Countries that had initiated (or were initiating) structural adjustment processes found that exchange appreciation interfered with the efficient attainment of trade liberalization goals and that price controls clashed with deregulation and privatization objectives.

Fiscal disequilibrium in an open economy has more immediate effects on the external balance, both in the current account (since there are no quantitative restrictions on imports) and, above all, in the capital account. The latter problem was accentuated in 1991 by heavy capital inflows, which exerted additional pressure on the exchange rate. Countries such as Chile and Colombia, which had opted for stable exchange rate parity, discovered the inefficiency of monetary policy in these circumstances and the necessity of fiscal overadjustment so long as the net capital inflows continue.

The Fiscal Impact of Trade Liberalization

Trade liberalization in Colombia in 1990 and in Argentina in 1988 caused a significant loss of fiscal revenue, owing to the characteristics and speed of tariff abatement, the process of exchange appreciation and the fact that both countries had based much of their previous fiscal adjustment on higher taxes on foreign trade.

Conversely, the characteristics of the existing protective structure and the nature and sequence of the deregulation process were such that in three of the countries studied, customs receipts remained constant or increased at the start of the trade liberalization and tariff abatement process. In fact, the elimination of exemptions (Chile in 1974-75), the replacement of nontariff restrictions with tariffs (Mexico in 1985) and the growth of the most heavily-taxed merchandise imports following the lifting of non-quantitative restrictions (Argentina in 1976-81) sparked an initial rise in the average effective tariff. This, together with the effect of the initial devaluation, led in three cases to an increase in customs receipts (as a percentage of GDP) at the start of the liberalization process.

This contrasts with the experience of most Asian countries and the situation of the small Latin American economies, whose protective structures are essentially tariff-based, so that tariffs are more important to the tax structure and the processes of liberalization initially caused a significant decline in customs receipts.

In the long term, and to the extent that liberalization results in low effective tariffs, it will be necessary in all cases to replace taxes on foreign trade with domestic taxes. Both the theoretical and the practical literature show that if fiscal equilibrium is to be maintained, an increase in the VAT (or the general sales tax) must accompany or precede trade liberalization. In other words, tariff reform and tax reform must be coordinated, as economic theory has always contended, but which so rarely occurs.

It is also found that in some small Latin American countries, the administrative costs and the characteristics of their economic structure rule out the total replacement of tariffs with taxes on domestic business activities.

Reform of the State and Fiscal Adjustment

Decentralization

The inevitable centralization of the collection of major taxes (income and VAT), together with the targeted decentralization of public spending, has significantly complicated fiscal adjustment in countries such as Argentina and, to a lesser extent, Colombia, necessitating the design of effective procedures for the transfer of resources. In particular, it is essential that revenue sharing not be based on a few taxes, since this leads to unwanted biases in the management of fiscal policy, and that appropriate incentives be considered for the territorial entities' own fiscal effort; otherwise, decentralization leads to deterioration of the overall elasticity of fiscal revenue, the growing reliance of territorial finances on transfers from the central government and, consequently, inordinate demands on central government finances.

Privatization

The study warns of the dangers inherent in using capital inflows from the sale of public enterprises and other public assets to achieve short-term fiscal equilibrium, instead of making permanent adjustments. The risks involved are very similar to those associated with the excessive external indebtedness which Latin American countries incurred in the latter half of the 1970s.

Tax Reform in Latin America

Tax reform in Latin America has been oriented toward the reduction of rates and the simplification of the individual income tax system; the abatement of taxes on capital earnings through the integration of company/partner taxation; the introduction of adjustments for inflation and the reduction of business tax rates; the widespread use of withholding, advance payment and presumptive systems; the generalized adoption of the VAT and the continued expansion of its coverage; and the elimination of numerous exemptions from direct and indirect taxes. Moreover, the initial use of quickly collected, easily managed taxes (on foreign trade, energy products and exchange and financial transactions) gave way in the late 1980s to the bolstering of basic tax receipts.

These reforms were prompted in particular by considerations of administrative simplicity, the need for resources in the wake of the fiscal crisis of the early 1980s, the impact of "supply-side economics" and, increasingly, the requirements of more open economies.

In the long term, the objectives of the structural reform process and, in particular, trade liberalization and financial deregulation, have revealed the need for increased receipts of basic taxes (income and VAT), as a result of:

• The growing conviction that a permanent and credible fiscal adjustment is necessary for the equilibrium of an open economy.
• The necessity of increasing or maintaining investments in human capital and physical infrastructure to improve the international competitiveness of the productive sector, which precludes continuing to base the fiscal adjustment on further cuts in public spending and, consequently, necessitates increased fiscal revenues.
• The temporary nature of the proceeds of privatization and the use and abuse of minor taxes that adversely affect economic efficiency.
• The potential need to replace taxes on foreign trade with domestic taxes and to avoid taxes on exchange and financial transactions, in furtherance of the trade liberalization and financial deregulation objectives.
• The need to generate fiscal surpluses to deal with the heavy inflow of capital that began in 1991.

Moreover, trade liberalization and financial deregulation have prompted efforts to boost income and VAT receipts, in particular through improved administration, expanded coverage, the reduction of exemptions and other concessions, the generalization of withholding systems and the use of presumptive systems, since only in this way can the dilemma of avoiding extremely high marginal rates while at the same time obtaining the fiscal resources needed for the above purposes be resolved. The recent trend toward stepping up administrative efforts in Mexico and Argentina is very instructive in this regard.

Generally speaking, recent trends have helped to improve the impact of the tax system on resource allocation in the economy. Nevertheless, there are still some concerns in this regard:

• In some countries, the economic structure and administrative capacity are such that the VAT has very different effects on the primary sectors, the manufacturing and service sectors, and on the formal and informal sectors. As the rates climb, the efficiency and resource allocation problems associated with this uneven impact increase in complexity.

• The recent trend toward the establishment of presumptive general income systems based on gross assets can create biases against new companies and increase the risk to which investors are exposed. Apparently, it would be better if these presumptive systems were based on net assets, as was the case initially in Colombia (1974) and Bolivia (1985).

Distributive considerations were missing from tax reforms in the 1980s. There is growing concern today, however, that this aspect of fiscal policy may have been unduly disregarded. Recent tax reforms in Chile and Colombia have addressed this subject.

Other topics that will gain importance in the fiscal debate in Latin America in the 1990s are (i) the coordination of tax policy and government subsidies in countries participating in the processes of subregional integration, and (ii) environmental taxes. Taxes on pollution and the deterioration of natural resources are, theoretically, the most efficient taxes. In industrialized countries these taxes are already a topic of public debate. The main problem is that a minimum level of international cooperation is required since, otherwise, countries that impose heavier environmental taxes may see their international competitiveness suffer.

An additional general conclusion is that although there are common trends and problems, tax reform and fiscal management must conform to the economic structure of each individual country and the macroeconomic circumstances in which it finds itself. *Omni et orbi* receipts are not efficient.

BIBLIOGRAPHY

Aninat, U.E. 1989. *Selected Policy Issues Concerning Personal Income Taxation in Mexico.* Working Paper. Aninat, Méndez and Associates, Economic Consultants. Mexico City.

Arellano, J.P., and M. Marfán. 1987. Veinticinco años de política fiscal en Chile. *Corporación de Investigaciones Económicas para Latinoamérica* 127:129–162.

Arrau, P., and D. Oks. 1992. *Private Saving in Mexico, 1980-90.* Washington, D.C.: The World Bank.

Aspe, P., and J.A. Gurria. 1992. Reform of the State and Economic Development: Thoughts from the Mexican Perspective. Paper presented at 1992 Annual World Bank Conference on Economic Development, Washington, D.C.

Baqueiro, A. 1991. *El déficit del sector público consolidado con el Banco Central: la experiencia mexicana de 1980 a 1989.* ECLAC-PNUD Regional Project on Fiscal Policy. Santiago, Chile.

Barkai, H. 1992. *Contours of Argentina's Macroeconomic Stabilization Strategy: 1989-1992.* Working Paper No. 135. Inter-American Development Bank. Washington, D.C.

Bartoli, G. 1988. *Fiscal Expansion and External Current Account Balance.* Working Paper. International Monetary Fund, Fiscal Affairs Department. Washington, D.C.

Basch, M., and E. Engel. 1992. *Shocks transitorios y mecanismos de estabilización: el caso chileno.* Working Paper No. 105. Inter-American Development Bank. Washington, D.C.

Beckerman, P. 1992. *Public Sector Debt Distress in Argentina's Recent Stabilization Efforts.* Washington, D.C.: The World Bank.

Bird, R. 1992. *The Tax Policy and Economic Development.* Baltimore: The Johns Hopkins University Press.

Bird, R.M., and O. Oldman. 1990. *Taxation in Developing Countries.* Baltimore: The Johns Hopkins University Press.

Blejer, M.I., and A. Cheasty. 1988. *The Fiscal Implications of Trade Liberalization.* Working Paper. International Monetary Fund, Fiscal Affairs Department. Washington, D.C.

———. 1987. *High Inflation, Heterodox Stabilization and Fiscal Policy.* Working Paper. International Monetary Fund, Fiscal Affairs Department. Washington, D.C.

Boskin, M.J., and C.E. McLure. 1990. *World Tax Reform: Case Studies of Developed and Developing Countries.* San Francisco: International Center for Economic Growth.

Bovenberg, A.L. 1989. *Tax Incentives and International Capital Flows: The Case of the United States and Japan.* Working Paper. International Monetary Fund, Fiscal Affairs Department. Washington, D.C.

Bruno, M., G. Di Tella, R. Dornbusch, and S. Fischer. 1988. *Inflación y estabilización: La experiencia de Israel, Argentina, Brasil, Bolivia y México.* Mexico City: Fondo de Cultura Económica.

Calvo, G., L. Leiderman, and C.M. Reinhart. 1992. *Capital Inflows and Real Exchange Rate Appreciation in Latin America: The Role of External Factors.* Washington, D.C.: International Monetary Fund, Research Department.

Carciofi, R. 1990. *La desarticulación del pacto fiscal. Una interpretación sobre la evolución del sector público argentino en las dos últimas décadas.* Working Paper No. 36. ECLAC. Buenos Aires, Argentina.

Carciofi, R., O. Cetrángolo, and G. Barris. 1993. *Reformas tributarias en Chile.* ECLAC Series on Public Policy Reform No. 9. Santiago, Chile: ECLAC.

Casillas, L. 1991. Ahorro privado, apertura externa y liberalización financiera en América Latina. Inter-American Development Bank. Washington, D.C. Mimeo.

Chu, K. 1987a. *External Shocks and Fiscal Adjustment in Developing Countries: Experiences During 1962-82.* Working Paper. International Monetary Fund, Fiscal Affairs Department. Washington, D.C.

————. 1987b. *External Shocks and the Process of Fiscal Adjustment in a Small Open Developing Economy.* Working Paper. International Monetary Fund, Fiscal Affairs Department. Washington, D.C.

Cline, W.R. 1992. *Argentina - Informe socioeconómico.* Washington, D.C.: Inter-American Development Bank.

CODEX Especial. 1992. *Reforma tributaria 1992.* Bogota, Colombia: Subdirección Jurídica Relatoria.

Dahl, H., and P. Mitra. 1991. Applying Tax Policy Models in Country Economic Work: Bangladesh, China and India. *World Bank Economic Review* 5:553-72.

Economic Commission for Latin America and the Caribbean (ECLAC). 1991. *La política fiscal en Colombia.* ECLAC-PNUD Regional Project on Fiscal Policy. Santiago, Chile.

————. 1990. "La economía de América Latina y el Caribe en 1990; la economía internacional; las finanzas públicas en la década de 1980." *1990 Economic Survey of Latin America and the Caribbean.* Volume 1. Washington, D.C.: United Nations.

Eyzaguirre, N., and O. Larrañaga. 1991. *Macroeconomía de las operaciones cuasifiscales en Chile.* Series No. 21. ECLAC-PNUD Regional Project on Fiscal Policy. Santiago, Chile.

Fanelli, J.M., R. Frenkel, and G. Rozenwurcel. 1992. Transformación estructural, estabilización y reforma del Estado en la Argentina. Paper presented at seminar "Stabilization Policies and Reforms of the State" sponsored by the Latin American Network for Macroeconomics. CEDES. Buenos Aires.

Farhadian-Lorie, Z., and M. Katz. 1989. Fiscal Dimensions of Trade Policy. In *Fiscal Policy, Stabilization, and Growth in Developing Countries,* M.I. Blejer and K.Y. Chu, eds. Washington, D.C.: International Monetary Fund.

FAUS/FESCOL. 1991 *Sistemas tributarios y ajustes por inflación en América Latina.* Bogota, Colombia: Editorial Nueva Sociedad.

FEDESARROLLO. 1990. *Coyuntura económica, análisis y perspectivas de la economía colombiana.* Bogota, Colombia: FEDESARROLLO.

Fernández, A.M., and R. Samaniego. 1986. *A Description and Analysis of the Structure of Fiscal Incentives to Industry in Mexico, 1983-85.* Working Paper. Instituto Tecnológico Autónomo de México. Mexico City.

Foxley, A. 1983. *Latin American Experiment in Neo-Conservative Economics.* Berkeley, Calif.: University of California Press.

Garay, L.J., and A. Carrasquilla. 1987. *Dinámica del desajuste y proceso de saneamiento económico en Colombia en la década de los años ochenta: ensayos sobre política económica.* Working Paper No. 11:5-72. Bank of the Republic, Economic Research Departament. Bogota, Colombia.

Gillis, M. 1989. *Tax Reform in Developing Countries.* Durham, N.C.: Duke University Press.

Giorgio, L.A., and R. Rivera. 1991. *Déficit cuasifiscal: el caso argentino (1977-89).* ECLAC Fiscal Policy Series No. 27. Santiago, Chile.

Go, D.S. 1990. Revenue Requirements of Stabilization, Structural Reform, and Growth. The World Bank Policy Research Department, Division of Public Economics, Washington, D.C. Mimeo.

Halevi, N. 1989. *Trade Restrictions and Reforms by Developing Countries in the 1980s.* Washington, D.C.: The World Bank.

Hanson, J.A. 1992. *Opening the Capital Account, a Survey of Issues and Results.* Working Paper No. 901. The World Bank. Washington, D.C.

International Monetary Fund. 1980-92. *Mexico, Recent Economic Development* (various issues). Washington, D.C.: International Monetary Fund.

———. 1992. *Argentina - Background Papers.* Washington, D.C.: International Monetary Fund.

———. 1990. *Tax Policy and Reform for Foreign Direct Investment in Developing Countries.* Working Paper. International Monetary Fund, Fiscal Affairs Department, Tax Policy Division. Washington, D.C.

———. 1989. *Argentina - Recent Economic Developments.* Washington, D.C.: International Monetary Fund.

Instituto de Estudios Fiscales. 1990. Sistema fiscal y administración tributaria. Análisis de dos realidades: España y Argentina. Madrid, España. Instituto de Asuntos Fiscales. Mimeo Document No. 80.

Inter-American Development Bank. 1992a. *Colombia - Informe socioeconómico.* Inter-American Development Bank, Economic and Social Development Department. Washington, D.C.

———. 1992b. *México - Informe socioeconómico.* Inter-American Development Bank, Economic and Social Development Department. Washington, D.C.

Ize, A. 1990. *Trade Liberalization, Stabilization and Growth: Some Notes on the Mexican Experience.* Washington, D.C.: International Monetary Fund.

———. 1989. *Savings, Investment and Growth in Mexico: Five Years After the Crisis.* Working Paper. International Monetary Fund. Washington, D.C.

Jenkins, G.P. 1992. Economic Reform and Institutional Innovation. Harvard Institute for International Development, International Tax Program, Cambridge, Mass. Mimeo.

Khalilzadeh-Shirzai, J., and A. Shah. 1991. Tax Policy in Developing Countries. Paper presented at World Bank Symposium. Washington, D.C.

Kigel, M.A. 1992. When Do Heterodox Stabilization Programs Work?: Lessons from Experience. *World Bank Research Observer 7(1):* 35-57.

Levy, P. 1992. *Chile - Current Macroeconomic Situation and Prospects.* Washington, D.C.: The World Bank.

Marcel, M. 1989. Privatización y finanzas públicas: el caso de Chile, 1985-88. *Corporación de Investigaciones Económicas para Latinoamérica 26:* 5-60.

Marcel, M., and M. Marfán. 1988. La cuestión tributaria. *Corporación de Investigaciones Económicas para Latinoamérica 13.*

Meller, P. 1992. *La apertura comercial chilena: Lecciones de política.* Santiago, Chile: CIEPLAN.

Mihaljek, D. 1992. *Tariffs, Optimal Taxes, and Collection Costs.* Working Paper No. 92/28. International Monetary Fund, Fiscal Affairs Department. Washington, D.C.

Mitra, P. 1990. *The Coordinated Reform of Tariffs and Domestic Indirect Taxes.* Working Paper. The World Bank. Washington, D.C.

Mitra, P., and D. Go. 1990. From India: Strategy for Trade Reform. In *The World Bank Report 8988.* Washington, D.C.: The World Bank.

Morley, S.A. 1992. *Policy, Structure and the Reduction of Poverty in Colombia, 1980-89.* Working Paper No. 126. Inter-American Development Bank. Washington, D.C.

Newbery, D., and N.H. Stern. 1987. *The Theory of Taxation for Developing Countries.* New York. Oxford University Press.

Ocampo, J.A. 1992. *Policy Structure and the Reduction of Poverty in Colombia, 1980-89.* Working Paper No. 126. Inter-American Development Bank. Washington, D.C.

Ocampo, J.A., and E. Revéiz. 1979. Bonanza cafetera y economía concertada. *Revista Desarrollo y Sociedad* 2:233-55.

Oks, D.F. 1992. *Stabilization and Growth Recovery in Mexico: Lessons and Dilemmas.* Washington, D.C.: The World Bank.

Oks, D.F., and D. Dunn. 1991. *Forecasting the Primary Fiscal Balance in Mexico.* Washington, D.C.: The World Bank.

Ortiz, G. 1990. Public Finance, Trade and Economic Growth: The Mexican Experience. In *Fiscal Policy in Open Developing Economies,* ed. V. Tanzi. Washington, D.C.: International Monetary Fund.

Ortuzar, P. 1986. *La reforma previsional de 1980: mitos y premoniciones.* Working Paper No. 71. Centro de Estudios Públicos. Santiago, Chile.

Ospina, S.J. 1991. *Lecciones de la política fiscal colombiana.* ECLAC-PNUD Regional Project on Fiscal Policy. Santiago, Chile.

Peña, A. 1991. *El déficit del sector público y la política fiscal en Argentina, 1978-87.* ECLAC Fiscal Policy Series No. 12. Santiago, Chile.

Perry, G. 1992a. El proyecto tributario - Excesos e inequidades. *Economía Colombiana* 331:11-15. Bogota, Colombia.

————. 1992b. *Política petrolera: economía y medio ambiente.* Bogota, Colombia: Centro de Investigaciones.

————. 1992c. *Reforma tributaria, estabilización y ajuste: la experiencia colombiana.* Washington, D.C.: Inter-American Development Bank.

Perry, G., and M. Cárdenas. 1986. *Diez años de reformas tributarias en Colombia.* Bogota, Colombia: Centro de Investigaciones.

Perry, G., R. Junguito, and N. Junguito. 1981. Política económica y endeudamiento externo en Colombia en la década de los setenta. *Revista Desarrollo y Sociedad* 6: 197-249. Bogota, Colombia.

Perry, G., and J.A. Rodríguez. 1991. Las finanzas intergubernamentales en la Constitución de 1991. Santiago, Chile: Universidad Católica de Chile/Instituto de Economía.

Piza, J.R., G. Perry, and E. Lora. 1990. *Debates de coyuntura económica, reforma tributaria.* Bogota, Colombia: Centro de Investigaciones.

Rajaram, A. 1991. *Tariff and Tax Reforms: Do World Bank Recommendations Integrate Revenue and Protection Objectives?* Working Paper No. 1018. The World Bank. Washington, D.C.

Riedel, J. 1992. *Public Investment and Growth in Latin America.* Working Paper No. 134. Inter-American Development Bank. Washington, D.C.

Rojas-Suárez, L. 1992. *From the Debt Crisis Toward Economic Stability: An Analysis of the Consistency of Macroeconomic Policies in Mexico.* Working Paper No. 92/17.

International Monetary Fund, Fiscal Affairs Department. Washington, D.C.

Ros, J. 1992. Ajuste macroeconómico, reformas estructurales y crecimiento en México. Paper presented at the Latin American Network for Macroeconomics seminar on stabilization policies and reforms of the state. CEDES. South Bend, Indiana.

Sadka, E., and V. Tanzi. 1992. *A Tax on Gross Assets of Enterprises as a Form of Presumptive Taxation.* Working Paper No. 92/16. International Monetary Fund, Fiscal Affairs Department. Washington, D.C.

Sánchez, M. 1993. *Privatization in Latin America.* Washington, D.C.: Inter-American Development Bank.

Sargent, T.J., and N. Wallace. 1985. Some Unpleasant Monetarist Arithmetic. *Federal Reserve Bank of Minneapolis Quarterly Review* 9:15-31.

Sarmiento Palacio, E. 1991. *La política fiscal en Colombia.* ECLAC-PNUD Regional Project on Fiscal Policy. Santiago, Chile.

Shah, A., and J. Slemrod. 1990. *Tax Effects on Foreign Direct Investment in Mexico.* Washington, D.C.: The World Bank Division of Public Economics.

Shome, P. 1992. *Trends and Future Directions in Tax Policy Reform: A Latin American Perspective.* Working Paper No. 92/43. International Monetary Fund, Fiscal Affairs Department. Washington, D.C.

Sobarzo, H., and C.M. Urzúa. 1992. *A Very Brief Note on Tax Reforms in Mexico, 1980-92.* Working Document. Colegio de México. Mexico City.

Tanzi, V. 1989. *Fiscal Policy and Economic Reconstruction in Latin America.* Working Paper. International Monetary Fund, Fiscal Affairs Department. Washington, D.C.

———. 1988. Tax Reform in Industrial Countries and the Impact of the U.S. Tax Reform Act of 1986. *Bulletin for International Fiscal Documentation* 42:51-64.

———. 1987. Fiscal Policy, Growth and the Design of Stabilization Programs. *Finance and Development, A Quarterly Publication of the International Monetary Fund and the World Bank* 24:15-17.

Tanzi, V., and M.I. Blejer. 1988. *Public Debt and Fiscal Policy in Developing Countries.* Working Paper. International Monetary Fund, Fiscal Affairs Department. Washington, D.C.

Tanzi, V., and K. Chu. 1989. *Fiscal Policy for Stable and Equitable Growth in Latin America.* Working Paper. International Monetary Fund, Fiscal Affairs Department. Washington, D.C.

Thirsk, W., and P. Marwick. 1990. *Lessons from Tax Reform: An Overview.* Washington, D.C.: The World Bank, Division of Public Economics.

Thomas, V., and J.D. Nash. 1991. *Best Practices in Trade Policy Reform.* Oxford: Oxford University Press.

Urzúa, C.M. 1991. *El déficit del sector público y la política fiscal en México, 1980-89.* ECLAC Fiscal Policy Series No. 10. Santiago, Chile.

Van Wisjnbergen, S. 1991. Debt Relief and Economic Growth in Mexico. *World Bank Economic Review* 5(3): 437-55.

Wiesner Durán, E. 1992. *Colombia: Descentralización y federalismo fiscal: informe final de la misión para la descentralización.* Bogota, Colombia: Presidencia de la República, Departamento Nacional de Planeación.

Williamson, J. 1990. *Latin American Adjustment: How Much Has Happened?* Washington, D.C.: Institute for International Economics.

World Bank. 1992a. *Colombia: Macroeconomic Consistency and Structural Reforms.* Working Paper No. 9764-CO. Washington, D.C.

———. 1992b. *Argentina: Public Finance Review - From Insolvency to Growth.* Washington, D.C.: World Bank Office for Latin America and the Caribbean.

———. 1991a. *Lessons of Tax Reform.* Washington, D.C.: The World Bank.

————. 1991b. *Colombia: Public Sector Expenditure Review.* Working Paper No. 7891-CO. Washington, D.C.

————. 1990. *Argentina - Política tributaria para la estabilización y la recuperación económica.* Washington, D.C.: The World Bank.

INDEX